Introduction

Paddy Kingsland was brought up in rural Hampshire in post war Britain. The soundtrack to his childhood was the BBC Light programme and later Radio Luxembourg. There were less than successful piano lessons accompanied by experiments with audio amplifiers and tape recorders. The purchase of a guitar in a junk shop led to village hall gigs followed by touring with a semi-pro band. Late nights, led to shocking A level exam results but thankfully the BBC was understanding about academic failure at that time, preferring enthusiasm and a genuine interest in the practicalities of broadcasting. They employed him as a technical operator aged eighteen.

Early work as an assistant engineer/tape editor, included a mixture of light entertainment and rock 'n roll; everything from Victor Sylvester to Gene Vincent.

A chance visit to the Radiophonic Workshop led to a temporary "attachment" to the unit at the BBC's Maida Vale Studios. This eventually led to a permanent post and in the ten years up to 1981 he wrote theme tunes for radio and TV, jingles for local radio, scores for radio drama, schools and children's TV, including "The Changes".

In the late 70s he wrote incidental music for several Doctor Who series, as well as Radio & TV versions of "The Hitch Hikers Guide To The Galaxy".

At the end of 1981 he left the BBC to set up a studio in Hammersmith, and continued contributing to to BBC programmes including Doctor Who as well as TV commercials, feature films and corporate videos.

The travel documentary Around The World In 80 Days led to a BAFTA nomination for best TV Music.

He made eight albums of library music for KPM which are in use worldwide.

In 2009 he joined colleagues from the BBC Radiophonic Workshop for a live concert at the Roundhouse. Since then the 'Band' has played at many festivals including Isle of Wight, Glastonbury, Blue Dot, End Of The Road and many more.

Other projects include 'Unreasonable Rhymes', a book of poems available from Amazon. Book 2 is on the way, together with 'All Still There', memories of a country childhood, to be published soon. "Listen For The Light", a collaboration with Nick Gomm, is an album of Sitar and electronics.

Rocking At the BBC (Still in love with Auntie) is an account of his time as a member of staff at the BBC between 1966 and 1981.

Contents

Rocking at the BBC

(Still In Love With Auntie)

By Paddy Kingsland

A personal memoir of the time I spent under the wing of "Auntie" BBC. Like all relatives she could be in turn loyal, protective, affectionate, illogical, utterly frustrating and annoying... but in the end a treasured friend.

For Lynda

Chapter 1: Evesham

…..hope all going well with the course. I expect so, no news is good news as they say. Not much to report here. Aunt Muriel not too well, so Terry is having to do the milking on his own. Hopefully not for too long. It seems a bit quiet here without you around. Mrs P. and I are going for walks as usual. Spring is just around the corner, the nights are getting shorter now. Look forward to seeing you when you have the long weekend. I know you're busy but let me know details when you can. Give me a chance to get food in!

Much love,
Mum

p.s. I miss you….

My poor Mother. I see that now but when I received that letter in January 1966 I was happily in residence at the BBC's Engineering Training Department at Evesham. It took me a few years to appreciate the effort she had made to help me get there. I was flying the nest and happy with my fresh start.
Technical Operator course number 24 - T.O. 24 - consisted of 21 like minded 19 year olds, most of whom had found other things to do while supposedly

studying for A level exams. We had been recruited to join the operational staff of BBC Radio in London. We were to be trained as T.O.s; technical operators. There were other courses going on for T.A.s, Technical assistants. These chaps adopted a rather superior attitude because we merely operated the equipment whereas they were able to take it to bits and repair faults. As one of them put it, their job was to repair the gear we had broken. We were expected to have made some sort of stab at A levels but more emphasis was placed on fitting into the team. They wanted manual dexterity, so hobbies like music and photography went down well, together with amateur dramatics, hi-fi and tape recording. Home computing was a distant dream then.

Just after Christmas on Monday the 3rd of January 1966 I had caught the train from Ropley station, having bought a ticket from the station master Mr Woodley, who was my friend Dave's dad. Dave together with most of my friends had gone off to college or university the previous September because while I had been playing in a band in the evenings they had been doing their homework and moved on to academic studies. Even with the roaring coal fire in the Station's waiting room the atmosphere was less than cheery. Our parents were very proud of us but sad to see us go. This was the end of a happy era for them. Without us and our guitars it would be very quiet. We didn't know it then but Ropley station itself had only a few years to go before it would be closed down.

Needless to say I was on top of the world to be leaving the sleepy village and speeding on my way to an amazing adventure. After a couple of changes at Winchester and Basingstoke I was on the train to Evesham together with (unknown to me) most of my future classmates.

On arrival at Evesham a few of us ended up a hundred yards past the end of the platform so we had to clamber off the train and trudge along the side of the track with our suitcases. An old green bus with the familiar BBC logo painted on the side was waiting outside the station to take us to Wood Norton, a few miles outside Evesham. Wood Norton Hall was once a stately home occupied by Prince Philippe, Duke of Orléans. The BBC bought it in 1939 to be used as a wartime broadcasting centre away from London in the event of Broadcasting house being bombed. Twelve radio studios were built in the house and grounds and by 1940, Wood Norton had become one of the largest broadcasting centres in Europe, producing over eight hundred hours of radio programmes a week. Many of these included coded messages for resistance fighters in Europe. After the war ended it became a training centre for engineers and operators in radio and television.

The ancient BBC bus chugged up the drive of Wood Norton Hall and Technical operator course number 24 alighted for the first time. Major Oldman, the officer in charge of welfare, was there to meet us and we were soon in a warm lecture room, suitcases piled up outside. The hall was a bit like a James Bond set with bundles of cables running everywhere, hung between the ornate ceilings and oak panelled walls. There were no preservation orders to hold up the work when the BBC took over the stately home in 1939. The Major welcomed us and dished out piles of paper, maps of the hall and grounds, timetables, canteen opening hours, cash office times, fire drill, BBC regulations, and so on. There was a brief warning about the standards of behaviour expected. The accommodation was segregated. Visits to the girls living in Pear Tree cottage were strictly forbidden. In those days it was not considered necessary to forbid the girls from visiting us. The Major informed us that he lived on site and was always 'available' if a problem arose....' Finally we were allocated rooms in the outside blocks. The rooms were clean but basic. Two beds, wash basin, wardrobe and two desks - homework was to be expected. Communal showers and loos, no TVs.

I shook hands with Nick Gomm who would share the room and we began to get to know each other. That process has continued to this day as we became lifelong friends through work, girl friends, break-ups, weddings, births and deaths. It turned out that we had similar backgrounds. Both of us were brought up in the country, passed the eleven plus and went to grammar schools. We both played guitars in groups and built amplifiers in garden sheds. We both spent the previous two 'A' level years not working for exams. Both of us had had no ambition to go to university and so this chance to work at the BBC was not to be messed up - we were both in the last chance saloon. Unpacking done and suitcases stowed under beds it was time to get something to eat. The first visit to a BBC canteen. Over the sixteen or so years I worked at the BBC there were few visible changes in the canteens. Same tables and chairs, same counter to slide same trays along, same ladies and chaps serving, same selection of food. Many years later I did a gig at an American airforce base which was like stepping into a New York diner. Every detail of decor, equipment and merchandise had been imported, right down to the last Hershey bar. Evesham's canteen was like that, a little bit of Broadcasting House dropped into the Worcestershire countryside There were always terrible jokes about BBC canteens from comedians and DJs but in reality the food was good and inexpensive. The system in those days was that the BBC paid for the infrastructure and staff, and the prices we paid covered the cost of the raw materials. I can't remember what I ate that evening but it was probably welsh rarebit and chips, maybe a pud but definitely tea. There were rumours that they put bromide in the tea to dampen the ardour of the randy among us. The total cost of the meal was under half a crown, twelve and a half pence in today's money. That might sound cheap but my first monthly pay cheque was about £32.

We met a few people on our course. They seemed very confident and with good reason. They had been working "on station" for the previous three months. The BBC was expanding at that time, BBC2 had started up and local radio was on the horizon. As people moved to fill the new vacancies in TV, new staff were required in radio. The ETD (engineering training division), could only cope with so many TO (technical operator) training courses and so those courses were filled with a mixture of new and slightly more experienced staff who had worked for a time at BH (Broadcasting House) or Bush, (Bush house). These new friends dazzled us with their command of the jargon. Everything seemed to have an acronym. EIC; engineer in charge, OBs; outside broadcasts, TC; Television Centre. Someone joked that there was a job in existence somewhere in the BBC of

E-I-E-I-O; occupied by a Mr MacDonald. A walk around the grounds revealed the extent of the ETD campus. Many prefab buildings, some used as classrooms, others as accommodation blocks. Some of these looked a bit smarter than our wartime units and were used for senior staff on more advanced courses.

One larger building was revealed to be a fully equipped TV studio with cameras, lights and everything! Amazing! Even more amazing was the monitor screen with a test card on it. In full colour. That was the first time any of us had seen colour TV and it would be over another year before it was first transmitted from the Wimbledon tennis tournament in 1967.

After a long day it was time to turn in; we needed to be in top form for a canteen breakfast the following morning. Showered and dressed in the brand new sports jackets the purchase of which had been supervised by our mothers, we went to the canteen. The place was full because all kinds of chaps on other courses had driven up from London late the previous night. Making our way past an assortment of flash cars owned by these characters, we made our way to a classroom for the first session. Most of us expected to launch straight into a talk on microphones, mixers and tape machines. But this was the BBC and so a good deal of bureaucracy needed to be completed before getting to the good stuff. Another welcome from the Major included details of recreational facilities nearby and an invitation to join the BBC club. This was a wonderful organisation with sections for almost everything imaginable from hockey, football and rugby to sailing, gliding and amateur dramatics. There was a sports ground at Motspur Park in South London and bars in almost all BBC premises serving drinks and food at way below pub prices. There was a subscription to pay but I never met a BBC member of staff who had not joined. The profits from drinks bought by non athletic members subsidised the hobbies of the sporty types. At that time drink featured heavily in the daily routine of most professions and the BBC was no exception. The bars in London and elsewhere were all full at lunch time and most people weren't drinking Perrier water. Attitudes have changed since then. There was no BBC club at Wood Norton hall, but one had been sensibly located in the town of Evesham. The old green bus obligingly chugged into the town every evening and ferried the drinkers back in full song, at 10 30.

> *Why were they born so beautiful*
> *Why were they born at all*
> *They're no bloody use to anyone*
> *They're T-O twenty four*

When the Major had finished his introductory remarks there was a more formal welcome from the head of engineering training department (HETD), Mr Mackenzie. In quietly menacing Scottish tones he reminded us that we were there to work and those who failed to make the grade would be severely dealt with.
"You've got to realise that if you do not put in the effort, you will be terminated". A representative of personnel department would come down from London to carry out the "terminations" of any backsliders who did not put in the work, leading to exam failure at the end of the course. This was a bit of a shock after the Major's soothing tones.

Then on a lighter note came a talk from Brigadier Prentice who advised the BBC on civil defence matters. This was in the era of the cold war. He gamely limped round the room telling us in plummy tones about the effects of a nuclear bomb falling on "Chairing Crawse station" and made less than helpful suggestions about the use of sandbags and other remedies for that eventuality.

After signing a terms of employment contract we also had to sign the official secrets act which was extremely exciting because it implied (wrongly), that we would be let in on some juicy privileged information.

Although health and safety was in it's infancy we got a first aid demonstration involving mouth to mouth resuscitation with a life sized doll called Resusci Annie. Very handy for reviving those who had had one too many in the BBC club. The rest of the day was spent meeting our lecturers, all experienced in the technical aspects of broadcasting and recording; from microphones all the way through to transmitters. They left us in no doubt that the course would be intensive we would need to keep up if we wanted to pass the exams in three months time. At the end of our first day we sorted out our ring binders of paperwork and after a canteen tea, boarded the bus to Evesham to sample the delights of the BBC Club for the very first time.

Chapter 2: E.T.D

Over the next 12 weeks at the BBC's Engineering Training Department we learnt about the 'broadcast chain'. All programmes went through many hands before reaching the listener. It might begin at an outside broadcast and travel over a post office, (now BT), landline to a continuity suite in Broadcasting House. In those days there were three networks, the Light programme, the Home service and the Third programme each of which had a continuity suite, consisting of a studio where a continuity announcer linked together the various programmes assisted by an operator in a control booth, who selected the various sources and controlled the sound levels. If anything went wrong it was the announcer's job to fill the gap in transmission with an apology and suitable music from a gramophone record.

From here the programme would go by another line to a transmitter many miles away; for example the long wave transmitter at Droitwich,. We were told that the signal from that transmitter was powerful enough to go round the world. It was possible put up an aerial nearby which could power a light bulb connected to it. In fact a local farmer had been found to be using this system to light up his cowshed free of charge. They told us that he was prosecuted for stealing electricity.

We were given very detailed notes for guidance on the volume of various programme types including news and talks, Big Ben, the shipping forecast, dance music, drama and even bagpipes. The aim was to make sure that programmes were properly balanced so that in an ideal world the listener would never be forced to adjust his volume control. This was not done 'by ear', but with reference to a meter, the Peak Programme Meter which displayed programme levels. The notes for guidance were prepared by a committee of five, whose signatures appeared at the end of that document. One of those was the head of presentation at the time John Snagge the very famous wartime announcer. In the final paragraph it was noted that "All have the right to query the volume of an incoming programme and such queries should not be resented or treated lightly." In spite of this we were soon to learn that a query about levels was often met with a terse "It's alright leaving me!"

Our lecturer at the time told us about a late night game played by some continuity operators. Transmitters are enormously powerful devices, their electrical outputs measured in millions of watts. If a sudden loud noise appeared during a programme it could damage the apparatus if left unchecked. That is why a safety device was in place to automatically shut down the transmitter in this event. The last item each night on the Home service was a record of a military band playing "God Save The Queen", before the network closed down for the night. So the game was to flick up the volume control at the very last moment and blow the transmitter off the air with the final chord of the music, without losing a note, a highly advanced manoeuvre which was guaranteed to annoy the transmitter engineers.

In earlier days, before tape recording came along, we would have been trained to record directly onto special gramophone disks, made of aluminium with a lacquer coating. This was an enormously skilled business. The cutting heads had to be accurately set so that the groove was deep enough to play back properly but not so deep that it cut into the aluminium. If that happened it was game over.   A spiral of waste, 'swarf' was created as the groove was cut which was removed by a vacuum device and fed into a bin. This was highly inflammable and a room was once burnt out when a careless producer put a cigarette end in the bin. A recording room or "channel" in those earlier days would contain two disk machines, recording at a speed of 78 or 33 rpm. with a maximum of five to twenty minutes of material. The operator started the first machine, then as that got to the end, set up the second machine and start it up, with a short overlap. Then take off the first disc, label it and set up a fresh disc. And so on. Imagine recording a Royal Wedding. And the horror of missing a bit. We had a lucky escape.

Our skills were to take a less technical but more creative turn with the use of recording tape which could be edited using razor blades and sticky tape. At its simplest an edit could be used to cut out a paragraph of speech in a discussion programme. More precise edits enabled music to be edited imperceptibly. And documentaries could contain thousands of cuts to create complex collages of material from different sources. Of course disc recording was still the medium for commercially released records because of the ease of duplication. And today vinyl is back, a return to albums with large format artwork and distinctive sound quality.

The three month course was intensive and included a lot of homework. Nick did me a favour by suggesting that we got up early each day and kept up with it. Neither of us wanted a repeat of our sixth form disasters. And there were frequent reminders that success in the end of course exams was the only route to continued employment. Auntie was firm on that point.

We still had a great time. Evesham is a beautiful part of the country and although January to March is perhaps not the best time to visit there were outings to pubs in quaintly named Upton Snodsbury and Wyre Piddle. The Beatles Rubber Soul provided the soundtrack for boozy nights at the BBC Club and there were movies in the big studio - Dr Strangelove and The Pink Panther. There were clandestine visits by some to Pear tree cottage to visit the four females on our course, hopefully avoiding the watchful eye of the Major.. The ratio of boys to girls on the course was 17 to 4 but if you took into account the hundred or so blokes on other courses, many of whom owned sports cars, the overall odds were not favourable.

As the end of March approached there were programme exercises. Full scale mock ups, some would say cock ups, of a real broadcasting network. Request shows, outside broadcasts from the rose garden, news flashes and so on. The artistic content was not judged as we took turns at being presenters, news readers and commentators. The matter in hand was getting the audio material 'on the air'. There was little chance of that with the instructors surreptitiously sabotaging our efforts. Fuses unexpectedly blew, plugs came out and phone lines mysteriously cut. It was all about "unflappability", working under pressure and a huge amount of fun was had by all although nerves played their part. At one point Mike Lucas appeared white faced and bleeding profusely. He had cut his finger on a razor blade during a tape editing test. He still passed but a few years later swapped to a career in personnel department or HR as it is now known. I wonder if he ever travelled up to Evesham to perform a termination? That is what was in store for four of our number who had not passed the final exams. But some of the others went on to greater heights. Gardeners Question Time producer and owner of a prominent production company, John Peel producer, Radio 2 executive, sound recordist for David Attenborough, sound engineers, including the one who brought us the soundtrack for Torvill and Dean's Bolero, East Enders cameraman, Human Resources executive and of course

Radiophonic operative. I and many others are grateful to Auntie for giving us that opportunity in the early part of 1966. I personally owe everything to that very fortunate beginning.

Chapter 3: London Calling

Three months flew past and the next step was moving to London where we would be sent "on station". I had not given this much, if any thought and was pleased when Chris Lycett approached Nick and me. "How about getting a flat together?" What a good idea that was. The BBC Welfare department was able to fix up temporary digs with landladies in London. Miss Twichet, (yes really), organised a room with a lady called Mrs Wisdom in Turnham Green. A large spare room, containing three beds, two gas rings and a sink. Bathroom along the landing, shared of course. On our first evening Chris had arranged to meet his brother at a pub nearby, the Chiswick Barge. Our first taste of swinging London with crowds of young people drinking outside on the banks of the river Thames. Chris's brother, a few years older than us worked at BH. (Broadcasting House). His attention was entirely focussed on the short skirted ladies, 'birds' in abundance, flocking to this trendy watering hole. He was in with a chance and we thought we were but in reality a bit young and obviously inexperienced. But spring was in the air in April 1966 and Spencer Davis was on the Jukebox singing 'Somebody Help Me' - Yeah! - life was good.

The following morning we all set off for our first day working at the BBC. Chris to BH, lucky chap and Nick and I to Bush House in the Strand, centre of overseas broadcasting known as the Tower of Babel with 42 languages transmitted on short wave all over the globe. The first job was to be interviewed by the bosses and allocated a shift. There were four groups, A,B,C & D to cover broadcasting 24 hours a day. The pattern was 4 evenings: 1600-2200, 4 days: 0900-1600, and 4 nights: 2200-0900. The nights required less staff and so some staff worked 'long days' instead, covering the meal breaks.

Mr Gibson was the EIC (Engineer in Charge) and new recruits were interviewed on arrival. He believed absolutely in the value of external services and impressed on us the high standards expected of us. He explained how the wartime broadcasts and later the BBC's coverage of the Suez crisis had made people the world over put their trust in the BBC. which had from time to time resisted pressure from government interference in order to give a balanced view. He mentioned that the Russians, envious of that reputation, had pointed out that the BBC had a clever knack of self criticism which lent credibility to their news bulletins. While Russian news broadcasts were sprinkled with references to glorious achievements of loyal comrades in their Tolyatti car factories, the BBC reported strikes by disaffected workers in Dagenham.

The next stage was 'shadowing" more experienced staff at work in the control room, tape editing channels and continuity suites. This meant watching others doing the job and fetching tea from the canteen in the basement until the senior staff reckoned we could be let loose on programmes.

However our main priority was to find a flat. Mrs Wisdom's room was a temporary measure and we wanted to be closer to the centre of London. The Evening Standard and the Evening News carried ads for furnished flats and at that time the demand exceeded supply. You had to be quick. Fortunately Chris's brother Tony had lived in London for a while and knew the ropes, so we benefitted from that experience. Chris picked up the papers, made appointments and phoned us with details of where to go. After a few failures we found a place in Westbourne Park Road W2. At least that's what the ad said but it turned out to be W11. Our new landlord Mr Lender insisted that the Post Office had got it all wrong and of course W2 sounded a bit more upmarket. But he liked the idea of 3 BBC salaries and we were in. Two rooms and separate shower/loo. We couldn't have stumbled into a better choice. The area was rough but colourful. Close to tube trains, less than an hour from work, near Portobello road with its market, tons of pubs, restaurants and people the same age as us. Lucy and Tina lived upstairs. Mr Lender often dropped in to 'adjust the gas fire' which made us all laugh. They were delightful and seemed to me to be over obsessed with new clothes, spending most of their earnings in Carnaby street at the end of the week. Like most young women at the time they were secretaries. Seems strange now that a generation of women equally or more intelligent than men were forced into a secondary role in offices because 'that's what girls did'.

Not all of course. The BBC had lots of women in other roles and this was as a result of the war. Up to 1939 all the engineering staff were male but many of them were called up to join the armed forces. Women were recruited to replace them because broadcasting was considered to be essential. The same was true for production staff but it would take a long time for women to make much progress in management. During my time at the BBC (60s & 70s), I was frequently working for women producers and although the system was not perfect I guess that there was a much greater atmosphere of equality in the BBC than elsewhere. Having said that, the female technical operators in 1966 were paid less than the men for doing exactly the same job. A few years later I met my wife Lynda at the BBC. She was a trained musician (unlike me), and had ambitions to play in an orchestra. In the end she decided to try for a job at the BBC when the first question asked was "Do you have shorthand and typing?" I am of course pleased that she said yes, or we would not have met but it led to her being shunted off into a clerical direction. During her time working as a secretary for David Epps, a music producer in Further Education, one of the contributors was Anthony Camden, a distinguished oboist with the London Symphony Orchestra and chairman of the board of that organisation. At that time the orchestra had a policy of being all male. He explained that the reason for this was the practical difficulty of touring with a large number of people. By sharing hotel rooms the accommodation costs were halved. Involving women complicated this arrangement. But auditions presented another thorny problem. Should potential recruits of both sexes play behind a screen so that appearance was not an influence? Things are different now and there are many more female players but as I write this it is still not 50/50. And Lynda had made a career mistake by taking up the flute, at least in the commercial sense. There are only four flute chairs up for grabs as against a possible sixty for the string section players. Many other orchestras at that time, including those at the BBC, did employ women.

Many years later I was asked to write a piece of music for schools TV to go with a cartoon to demonstrate changing tempos, or tempi as I ought to say for the musically educated. The cartoon showed a cat chasing a mouse and the music needed to follow the action as the pace sped up and slowed down. The idea was to film a conductor and musicians in the studio, recording the cartoon music track to show how this worked. We asked a fixer to book the band for the BBC. It was, as always, assumed that the best available session players would be called first. When this was done the producer contacted me and said "These are all men! What kind of a message does this give to the children watching?" I was shocked because it simply hadn't occurred to me. There was an established pool of players working on sessions, most of whom at that time were men. We changed the line up accordingly adding female players who were of course at least as good as the men. My only defence is that it was a case of unintentional entrenchment. And worse still I have only just got around to wondering why nobody suggested a female conductor.

Meanwhile back in 1967 we were all having a great time working at the BBC, living in Notting Hill on very little and going to parties whenever possible. The standard procedure on Saturday nights was to buy a bottle of Bulmers Woodpecker cider or a 'Party Four' (pint) beer tin and ring the bell of a flat with loud music playing - "We're friends of Steve's..." combined with the booze usually got you in.

The hope was to "get off with" a girl. The swinging sixties. I don't know what I was doing wrong apart from being 19 years old and not owning a Triumph Spitfire... but I had no luck in that area. Unlike my flat mates for a while, probably until I stopped trying too hard. What happened in 183 Westbourne Park Road stays there but it was by no means all bad. Those were the days. Our own parties were a huge success because we had amazingly loud amplification together with the latest releases cut together using our tape editing skills. Jimi Hendrix & Tamla Motown could be heard for miles which of course attracted gatecrashers, sometimes holding up bottles of Woodpecker cider.

Nick and I had our guitars and soon formed a band. A drummer joined us, John Lightfoot was an engineer at TV Centre and we practiced in our small flat. We were soon joined by Roger on electric piano and bass player Luke. We even managed to get a few gigs at school hops and the like. We had some black and white pictures done in which it was totally forbidden to smile. Menacing was the order of the day. We needed a name and Roger who was working in publishing suggested Gog Magog. I still have no idea what that was all about. But it was fun until Luke vanished suddenly leaving us bass-less. We had a booking the following week and needed someone to fill in. It was suggested that we should go the Ship pub in Wardour Street where musicians hung out. We did so, failing to look particularly cool. Somebody directed us towards a guy at the bar "Johnny's a bass player…" We plucked up courage and approached him. He did look cool and spoke with a Liverpool accent. Pretending (unconvincingly) to be established rock 'n rollers we invited him to a rehearsal and a gig.

He accepted straight away but added that he would need to be picked up with his gear. Our drummer John, owner of a mini van, agreed and Johnny resumed his conversation at the bar. A few days later John went to pick him up at an Earls Court flat. When the door opened John said "Hi I've come to pick up Johnny". The response from Johnny was "He's out". He was clearly in temporary financial difficulties and avoiding the rent collector. This fabulous musician was Johnny Gustafson during a lean patch after his time with Liverpool groups The Big Three and The Merseybeats, etc. If it hadn't been a lean patch he certainly wouldn't have been playing with us. Misunderstanding resolved, they arrived at our Westbourne Park Road flat complete with Johnny's friend Dave. After setting up the gear we went through a couple of our numbers which went ok, then Johnny suggested he sang something. Good idea. River Deep and Mountain High? OK. How about if Dave has a go on drums? This suggestion was fine for Nick and me but our drummer John looked doubtful. Well… alright… Dave sat at the kit and made a few adjustments. They launched into the number at super high volume. Johnny's clear high voice and throbbing bass line together with an amazing thrashing drum part from Dave with all the stops and accents perfect, Nick and I joined in bravely but added very little. Even so it was the most amazing musical experience of my life. The silence that followed the last chord was broken by a tinkle as part of John's snare drum rolled away. Dave's energetic tour de force had been too much for the beloved Premier kit. At least that gave John an excuse to be annoyed, as Dave sat with a rueful expression. Needless to say that the gig went ok the following week, (minus Dave), and we all got to experience playing with a real rock star. Johnny went on to greater things - he is easy to find on the internet - but sadly passed away in 2014. As for John our drummer, he and I went on to start a mobile disco, of which more later, but a few years afterwards he ended up in a very senior post in BBC TV. Like Nick he is still a great friend and the three of us meet once a year to play through the old numbers. That's a thought, we must try River Deep And Mountain High next time. I wonder if Dave is available?...

Chapter 4: The Tower Of Babel

The polished brass plate at the entrance to Bush House announced that the BBC External Services broadcast in over forty languages from the building. Known as the Tower of Babel by more cynical observers Bush House was a poor relation. It was funded not from the license fee but a direct grant from the government which encouraged it to sponge off other BBC departments which were funded by the license fee and intended to cover the costs of providing broadcasting in the UK. Editorial control did however remain with the BBC. But it wan't easy to control translators ranting their political views in a foreign language in overnight broadcasts, which happened more than once. More entertainingly I remember a punch up in the canteen involving Arab and Israeli production staff. This was fortunately before mobile phones were around because Fleet street was just around the corner.

There were many interesting characters at Bush House. and Margot Davies was one of them. Slightly eccentric, definitely from a posh background, fragile and charming. She was the freelance producer in charge of 'Calling Newfoundland'. She spent far more time and effort preparing her material than the small fees could realistically justify. But what was most striking about her was the kindness she showed to people less fortunate than herself. There were quite a few homeless people on the embankment close to Bush House and she went further than simply throwing coins into their collecting tins. She took them with her to have a meal in the canteen and was interested in their stories. I remember joining her at a table where she was entertaining a rather shy man who was eating a meal. She explained how he had been an airman during the war. He had little to add to this but she treated him with respect and interest as if he were an old friend, which I suppose he could have been. She later explained that he had tried to live in proper accommodation but couldn't face the complications and preferred to live on the streets. His wartime experiences had taken their toll and he was unable to cope with the responsibilities of renting a flat. There were many similar stories about her kindness. She was brave too because the embankment was not the safest place at night. But she is one of the few truly good people I have met in my life.

Another name which sticks in my mind for rather different reasons is Mr Akram Sali. Anyone working at Bush in those days will recognise this name because he was constantly being paged on the Tannoy in both the canteen and the BBC club bar. "Calling Mr Akram Sali in box one…" was the soundtrack to lunch, dinner and tea breaks. The telephone switchboard operators had to pronounce similarly exotic names every day as they sought those who were either out of the office or wanted urgently in the studio. Many of the translators/presenters had complex love lives and it was suspected that the urgent need to track them down was not always related to their broadcasting activities. On one famous occasion a joker rang the switchboard and asked for Mr Sex Maniac to be paged in the canteen, emphasising the letter i making the word sound foreign. The operator obligingly paged "Mr Sex Maniac in box one…" - then as the penny dropped "Ohhhh… This received a round of applause from the diners in the canteen. Needless to say nobody made their way to box one…

Ron Farrow produced religious programmes for the World Service and had the type of sense of humour which led to him make spoof calls to his secretary, claiming to be a celebrity or even royalty. One day when the phone rang the long suffering girl answered and asked who was speaking. The caller replied "The Archbishop of Canterbury". "Oh shut up Ron!" she cried before realising the call was genuine…

A feature of being new recruits was that we were encouraged to make use of empty studios to play at making radio shows and practice recording, mixing and editing. There were a number of unofficial creative efforts during the night shifts. One skilful editor managed among other things to change 'The British Broadcasting Corporation' into 'The British Broadcorping Castration. The same team made a hysterical version of a current pop song called "They're Coming to Take Us Away" based on the horrors of working at Bush House. My flatmates Nick, Chris and I moved into the drama studio which was quite large and unused in the evenings. We recorded our band and were joined from time to time by various musicians, one of them a young Roger Limb, who later joined the staff of the Radiophonic Workshop.

The BBC external service was all about news, current affairs and journalism. Eyes shone when the yearly political conferences came round in the Autumn. The Aberfan disaster in 1966 and the six days war in '67 sent the place into overdrive. For some people this was an exciting place to work, supporting the journalists getting their work onto the air. But I wanted more than that and I envied flatmate Chris who was working at Broadcasting House on entertainment shows. I remember meeting for lunch one day and going to studio 2 in the basement of BH where he was in a recording booth attached to the mixing room. A small orchestra was playing in the studio, visible through a glass window. The excitement I felt every time I heard live music came back and I was enthralled in the same way as I had been as a child when my parents took me to a pantomime at the Kings Theatre Southsea. There was no turning back. I was desperate to escape from Bush house and be part of this exciting world.

A re-organisation of staff was going on at the time, (when isn't there in the BBC?), so that Technical Operators were to be absorbed into the programme operations department. In other words here a chance to move into the studios. The alternative, unthinkable for me, was to remain in a more technical role in the control room. Time moves more slowly when you are 20 and it seemed to take ages to get through the necessary interviews to be declared fit to become a "POA". A programme operations assistant, the new name for SMs (Studio Managers). Why that changed defies reason but in due course I was presented with a leather briefcase to hold editing kit (razor blades chinagraph pencil and sticky tape), scripts and cigarettes - I had rather foolishly started smoking but everyone seemed to be doing it so... and armed with that briefcase I was told to go and watch what went on in the studios at Bush house. Goodbye to Engineering Division, hello Programme Operations department. For me this was a step in the right direction. After a training course at the Langham (a BBC building opposite Broadcasting house, formerly a hotel, I was back at Bush house working in studios.

After the production staff had done their stuff quite a few technical people were needed to put the programmes on the air. BBC domestic broadcasting within the UK in the early 60s consisted of three networks. The Light programme, the Home service and the Third programme. Assuming that the programmes arrived from a studio, an OB (outside broadcast) or a tape, these elements still needed assembling before sending them off to the transmitters. This was largely done in the three continuity suites each with an announcer and an operator to make sure all the transitions were smooth and sound levels correct. They were also able to deal with breakdowns and be flexible about timings if the news overran. So assuming three shifts you needed at least six people per network per day to staff this. But at Bush house there were many separate broadcast chains transmitting to audiences all over the world in over forty languages. The idea of a continuity announcer for each language was unrealistic. A more economical method was needed, and so an automatic switching system was devised for Bush House. The programme junctions happened at exact times so accuracy was required from those working in the studios. On one night shift I was in a studio for a Bengali transmission. The order of events for me was to switch on the mic when the red transmission light came on and make an announcement in English (fortunately). Next play a taped theme tune, fade it down and cue the newsreader in the studio who would speak from a script for about 12 minutes. Nothing to do during that time after which fade out the newsreader, bring in the music and then make a closing announcement to introduce the next programme after which at an exact time the transmission would automatically switch to the next studio. Simple. That is the theory of what was meant to happen except that it was 3 o'clock in the morning and at some time during the presenter's twelve minute reading I (understandably) nodded off. I woke to the sound of the newsreader banging on the glass window which separated the studio from the control cubicle shouting "wake up, WAKE UP!". This was all being transmitted to the listeners until I hastily turned off his mic. I started the music tape and mistakenly began reading out the opening announcement. Time was running out and I switched to the closing announcement at breakneck speed just before being cut off. I don't know how many listeners in India heard that display of incompetence but I hope it amused them more than the (probably dull) news broadcast that preceded it.

The newsreader left without comment just as the phone rang. The engineer in the main control room was still laughing as he said "Shame about the snoop tape!" Snoop tapes were recordings made of some broadcasts for reference purposes. Checking up on the night shift. It had been known for newsreaders to read out propaganda for political reasons. My acquaintance in the control room decided this tape was not very important and so it got accidentally mangled as it was rewinding. Disaster averted with grateful thanks. Restorative coffee and welsh rarebit in the canteen required.

The others in the flat could drive but had no money to get cars. My mum offered me a choice for my 21st birthday. A party or a hundred quid. I went for the hundred quid and bought a third hand Triumph Herald. The car was for the time being based at her house and I started driving lessons with a retired army instructor during time off at home. I had already failed a test for which I was totally unprepared. Another test was booked and my army major instructor arrived the day before for a last lesson before my triumphant graduation into the wonderful world of driving independence. The lesson went OK and the Major ended the lesson with a request to see the test appointment card. "It's tomorrow at four" said I. "Let me see the card please" replied the Major with military precision. The 16th at 4 PM. "That's today!" said the Major. "And it's 4 pm now. We'll never make it in time." Oh dear… I passed eventually and the Triumph Herald joined the party in London. Not long after that I crashed it into a brick wall in Wimbledon, fortunately unhurt, but that lesson has remained with me to this day.

Chapter 5: BH

I soon started a campaign to get a transfer from Bush House to the glamour of Broadcasting house. You may think they would have been glad to get rid of me but at the time it seemed ages before that happened. At last I was sent to BH - Broadcasting House in Portland Place. This was my dream because I was desperate to work on programmes that people wanted to listen to. Shows that gave people pleasure. It never really felt as though anyone was listening to the output of Bush House although I suppose they must have been… my first live show was Housewives Choice, and the programme's title is an illustration of how much things have changed since then. It came from one of the studios in the basement of Broadcasting House, a daily request show on the Light Programme every weekday at ten past nine after the news.

There were four of us in the control room, a producer, a secretary a more senior studio manager - the panel SM who controlled the sound levels and me. My job was to play in the "Gramophone" records, oh.. and get the teas from the canteen.

In the studio, separated from us by a large glass window sat the presenter, in this case the well known comedian Ted Ray. When the time came for refreshment he presented me with a ten shilling note (50p), He would have had plenty of change because a round of teas and coffees cost under three shillings then, fifteen pence in today's money. The second hand of the big studio clock was ticking up to ten past nine and the panel operator switched the loudspeaker over to the output of the Light Programme. How exciting! The continuity announcer made the introduction which was my cue to play the theme tune. Even though I had done this perfectly a hundred times at Bush House, this was to me the real thing. My hands were shaking - My Mum would be listening! Unfortunately, wanting to be slick, I had lined up the beginning of the record too close to the stylus and the tune "wowed" in, not an auspicious start to my new job. Fortunately the rest of the show went OK but it was an early warning about attention to detail.

After working on general programmes for a while I was transferred to Group A - pop music and light entertainment. Flatmate Chris had been there for a while now. Radio One had just started and one of the shows he had worked on was the John Peel programme on Sunday afternoons. Most of the new DJs from pirate radio worked in the self operated continuity suites, surrounded by record decks and jingle cassette players, putting the shows together themselves with their own brand of flashy manual dexterity. Kenny

Everett was the king of this technique. When John Peel started in Radio One he used to do his shows with a more traditional set up. He sat in a studio and did the links while an SM in the control room played the records and tapes on cue.

Nick and I sometimes (enviously) listened to the show at home before we were transferred to broadcasting house.

On one occasion I asked Chris about a record I had heard on the show but had missed the name of the artist. The following week Chris asked John Peel and instead of just giving the name he wrote a note with full details and a couple of recommendations for similar tracks. How nice of him to take the trouble to do that. I think he was genuinely pleased to introduce people to new things and continued to do that for many years.

Nick was into graphology at the time and was keen to have a go at John Peel's handwriting. I gave him the note and I'm afraid I have forgotten what his findings were except that they were surprising (to us), but all good.

I had always assumed that everything happened at broadcasting house but the BBC had lots of other buildings in use in central London, the nearby Langham hotel, Egton house and Yalding house mostly containing production offices, and there were various studios connected to BH by post office landlines buried under the streets. The Playhouse Theatre near Charing Cross, The Paris Cinema in lower Regent street, the Camden theatre, Maida Vale, the Grafton theatre and the Piccadilly. These were our playgrounds. Most of the shows with audiences were made in these studios. Jazz Club, John Peel concerts for Radio 1, comedy shows, quizzes, even, bizarrely, dance shows. On the radio? Yes, Victor Silvester and his ballroom orchestra played foxtrots in strict tempo while a smartly turned out audience danced on the parquet floor. The shuffling and humming came over beautifully to an audience perhaps no longer able to enjoy the experience at first hand. But radio dancing was about to shuffle off as television offered a new dimension to this idea which is popular to this day. There were live lunch time pop shows with big bands like the Joe Loss Orchestra with guest groups and singers from the charts. Ballrooms still operated all over the country featuring resident big bands, however discos were beginning to take over.

Two audience shows which stick in the memory are Jazz Club and Country meets Folk, both broadcast live and transmitted from the beautiful Playhouse theatre in Northumberland Avenue.

At the back of the stalls a control room had been built together with a recording room but more or less everything else had been preserved. Red plush seats, the red stage curtains, and amazingly, under the stage the original machinery with wooden cogs and wheels for creating effects with traps and lifts, frozen in time until the BBC left several years later and the theatre was revived. There was a dress circle and even an upper circle, with seats all covered, patiently waiting to be used once again. I only remember the stalls being occupied by the "invited audience". These were regulars, fans of country music or jazz or whatever was on. Humphrey Lyttleton who was the Jazz Club compere often commented on the clientele - "Looking around this glittering audience..." The reality was that the whole front row was sometimes occupied by homeless people escaping from the cold, so that warming up the audience took on a whole new meaning. Admission was free but controlled by ticket unit who posted off tickets to anyone who applied. The commissionaires would be kind to the freezing characters without tickets and looked the other way. It's hard to believe that security was so relaxed in those days and very sad that nobody can be trusted in these times. But the jazz players were brilliant, in particular the sound of Tubby Hayes with his big band still rings in my ears. As there was no need for tight security the commissionaires were generally friendly and helpful. Some had retired from other jobs and were lively individuals. Johnny Johnson had been a head waiter at a top restaurant (with photos to prove it), and was a real laugh. A smart Rolls Royce limo had drawn up at the door to Maida Vale studios one afternoon and quite by chance I drew in behind it in my battered vehicle. Johnny ran out from the reception desk dressed in the full getup including cap and gloves. Instead of attending to the occupants of the Rolls he opened my car door and ushered me in with a smart salute, totally ignoring the celebrities.

Country Meets Folk was a regular Saturday show on Radio One. Featuring a mixture of Folk and

Country music with visiting American artistes, as well as musicians from all over the UK and Ireland with an audience at the Playhouse theatre. Flatmate Chris was lucky enough to be mixing the show and he got Nick and myself in to do the running around, playing in records, etc. It was a fun show and even more fun afterwards at the Ship and Shovel pub round the corner. We met talented Irish singer Hedley Kay there and he later became a regular performer on the show accompanied by Brian Brocklehurst a bass player originally from the jazz world. A highlight for me was a special show recorded at the Camden theatre with Buck Owens who was touring the UK with his band of top Nashville musicians. Watching them in action was a revelation. Gene Vincent came to do a recording session, no audience this time. He was delightful but sadly suffering very badly with an injured leg. He sounded great and was pleased with the vocal sound for which we rigged up a tape echo. It so happened that the design of the tape machine we used gave exactly the right effect for 'Be Bop A Lula'. Before my time Chuck Berry came to record for Saturday Club but wouldn't start until he was paid. In cash. And a busker called Don Partridge had a hit record called 'Rosie' was booked to appear but turned up very late because the money from busking that day in Trafalgar Square was so much better than the BBC fee. I remember recording a Ken Dodd show and almost running out of reels of recording tape because he carried on telling jokes long after the show was scheduled to finish.

Nobody complained and his lady friend sat in the front row meticulously noting reactions to the gags so that the act could be refined later on for maximum effect. It was a lesson to see how much hard work and attention to detail was put in by performers even when at the top of their game.

Broadcasting is team work and relies on a group of people to pull together to make a programme work. And I don't just mean the production team, for instance a session at the Playhouse involved four of those in the control box. But a tiny canteen with two or three tables was tucked away upstairs and in my day an elderly lady called Christine made tea and sandwiches for musicians and production staff. She was a delight and everyone adored her as she dispensed simple delightful goodwill with the refreshments. Everyone works better in a happy relaxed place. Sad to say she was robbed on the way home one night and her purse was stolen. Who would do that to a frail old lady? An immediate whip round restored the cash but a bit of the spark was extinguished that night.

Many more people behind the scenes oiled the wheels of the studios, commissionaires at the door, studio attendants moving the mics around, audience staff checking the tickets and ushering and of course the maintenance engineers in case the mixing desk exploded. We worked on a huge variety of shows. Doctor Finlay's Casebook was a successful TV series which transferred to Radio with the original cast and for some reason was produced by light entertainment department. I did the spot effects for a few episodes, doors opening, telephone rings, drinks poured etc, in the studio with the actors. It seemed strange working so closely with the actors I had often seen on the telly at home before I came to London. Rehearsal in the morning and recording after lunch. Andrew Cruickshank who played Doctor Cameron was getting on in years and used to have a lie-down after lunch before performing brilliantly and it was wonderful to work for the people I had grown up listening to, just as, sadly and inevitably they were on the way out. Max Jaffa, The Joe Loss band, Victor Silvester, comedians Al Reid and Jimmy Edwards.

Times were different then and quite a bit of alcohol was drunk before and after the shows. We were even allowed to claim RREs - "reasonable reciprocal expenses" to buy a drink in the pub for artists in the lunch break or after the show. All very sociable but frowned on now. I often wonder whether what we produced was better or worse for working under the influence.

This was the beginning of the end for mixed programming in radio. Everything was changing because streaming had arrived, not as we understand the word today but in the sense that the four new networks - Radios 1, 2, 3 & 4 - each had separate identities concentrating on pop music, light music. classical music and speech. And over the years as times change, what used to be light music eventually becomes the dated stuff that your auntie listened to. And what was once pop becomes the new light music.

In the sixties the musicians union had a needle time agreement with the BBC to protect work for musicians. This restricted the number of commercial records played in programmes. The rest of the music had to be performed by musicians in BBC studios. This meant that there was a constant stream of sessions for bands and groups. The results weren't bad considering, but recording several numbers including an attempt at recreating a hit single which had taken hours of studio time to perfect is a bit of a tall order in three hours. Unlike commercial studios the BBC was not as well equipped and did not have multitrack tape recorders at that time. The old school bands didn't have any problems because they turned up with perfect arrangements and sight reading musicians. On one occasion I worked on a session with the Sid Philips band who played superb dixieland jazz. The drummer looked a bit young and it turned out he was Sid's son. He played superbly, sight reading the parts but Sid kept him on his toes throughout the session, "Too loud Simon…etc" But this attention to detail obviously paid off because Simon later became a top rock drummer. I have come into contact with him a few times since then, a really gifted player.

The generation of Studio Managers before me had many talented sound mixers producing great mono sound for radio.

Freddy Harris was beginning to look elderly in 1969 and I remember a young rock band looking apprehensive as he carefully fiddled with the microphone positions, roll-up fag in mouth, before standing and listening intently to the sound they made in the studio. When they came into the control room to listen to the take they had just recorded their reservations soon vanished. Instant smiles. Freddy really knew what he was doing and loved his work. It was sad to see that he knew he would soon be reluctantly retiring. Joe Young was Jazz club's mixer in chief and could work magic with an intuitive ear for balancing music, particularly jazz. Robin Sedgley and Peter Ritzema were younger, talented mixers and also very funny. In the studio one of the band members was attempting to ingratiate himself with the producer. Stepping up to a mic he said "When's the last time we worked with you man? Quick as a flash the talkback key was pressed: "This is". On another occasion one of the band reacted to the demands for retakes they considered to be unnecessary with "Why can't we have … (the name of a female producer who was not quite so fussy) and once again over the talkback - "Why not? - Everybody else has…. Freddy and Joe stayed on as sound balancers until retirement but both Robin and Peter moved on to became producers. I have only mentioned a few but the department was full of talented and often witty people working in the music studios. It was a fantastic job and there were actually very few cross words. The performers were almost all considerate and friendly towards us junior staff but they must have been aware that the person pressing the buttons on the tape machine today may be producing the show and hiring the talent in a couple of years time. This was certainly true for flatmate Chris Lycett who after a successful mixing career went on to be a producer and ended up as head of production for Radio One. Nick Gomm the other flatmate went on to be a senior sound balancer and remained happily in that job until he retired although he always kept up his band activities, singing and playing regularly. Many people moved on from programme operations to production jobs in radio and TV. Too many success stories to mention them all. Some left to work as freelancers. John Etchells left the BBC to work as a recording engineer and producer with Joni Mitchel, George Harrison, Spandau Ballet, Queen and many others.

Maggie Rodford left to produce soundtracks for movies and commercials and is a leading figure in that field. There is no doubt that working as a studio manager at the BBC is a very good place to start a career.

Chapter 6: Rocking at the BBC

Scene and Heard was a pop magazine programme which went out on Radio 1 at lunchtime on Saturdays. The hour long programme was recorded on Thursday and Friday. My friend Nick Gomm and I were the regular technical team. We were, at the risk of seeming immodest, very good at tape editing and assembling features with music. The presenter Johnny Moran interviewed many visiting Americans keen to plug their records on Radio 1. Roy Orbison came in and talked about the early days. He was present at the recording of Great Balls Of Fire by Jerry Lee Lewis. In those early days at Sun studios in Memphis when they all hung around during each others sessions. The tape ran continuously and they kept the good bits. That day it wasn't quite working until the guitar player left to take a leak. When he returned they were coming to the end of another take of the song. He just played the final four chords. "Da Da Da Dah - "That's the one! - If the loo flushing had been recorded they would have kept it in. It is often said "It's not what you put in, it's what you leave out".

Journalists from the music papers often went to the stars with a portable recorder and brought back their tapes to be edited into the show. One of the journalists had an "in" with the Beatles and on one occasion he went to interview John Lennon but had only taken one reel of tape. Yoko Ono was there and wanted to take part - our journalist was worried about running out of tape and took to pressing the pause button during her lengthy interjections. Sadly they caught him at it and threw him out, which was the end of that particular "in". David Bowie came in wearing a dress, slightly offbeat even then, and a journalist who had given a glowing review of the test tone on a promotional pressing of John and Yoko's 'Wedding Album" in a music publication, was mercilessly reminded of it several weeks running by a witty competitor.

We often finished early on Scene and Heard and the producers used to wheel in Jimmy Savile to record his links for his Savile's travels show. I never understood why he was so successful and I have to say he gave me the creeps at that time. There were rumours about him, but then there were rumours about a lot of people. Times have changed and I have no doubt that in today's world he would have been found out.

Some of the producers and technicians played instruments and pretty soon Nick and I got invited to do gigs in spare evenings. Steve Allen was a producer for Radio 2 and ran a dance band for functions. He played the trumpet ok, but his real talent was as a compere. In those days the old standards were in demand, waltzes, foxtrots, cha cha etc, with a few rock and roll numbers thrown in. Steve sang the old songs (the cavalcade of crap as he referred to them) and his good natured humour worked a treat for any occasion. From Vidal Sassoon's Christmas bash at at the Cafe

Royal (or was it the Carlton Towers?) to East end weddings which always seemed to end in a punch up. There were quite a few Christmas parties at the Cafe Royal. These involved several recurring nightmares, starting with being turned away by the smartly uniformed doorman at the front entrance: "Tradesmen at the back door." Reload guitar and amp into car and drive round to the back. Via Piccadilly Circus one way system etc, etc. Now at the back door, fight your way to the function room, VIA THE KITCHENS!! This may sound easy but believe me it's not, as the well drilled staff are eager to give a hard time to any interlopers. Dump the gear on the stage and return via similarly hostile kitchens. With luck no parking ticket (or worse still no car), and find parking space. Again, sounds easy but this was a hundred yards from Piccadilly circus two weeks before Christmas. At last, return via front entrance (no tell tale tradesman's equipment), and a well earned drink at the bar with fellow band members, all totally unruffled. Is it just me?

The piano, bass and drums would turn up around 6pm to play background music while the dinner was served. That would be Jimmy Grant, a legendary radio producer and great pianist, Also composer of the famous Saturday Club theme tune. Laurie Monk, producer of Jazz programmes, ex trombone player for Ted Heath but now on bass guitar and Bryant Marriot, at that time assistant head of Radio 2 on Drums. The rest of the "orchestra" was booked for 8pm to play music for dancing when the tables had been cleared away and suitable amounts of alcohol consumed by the diners. The additional personal were Steve on trumpet, a saxophone player, and me on guitar and vocals.

On one occasion Bryant had to attend a last minute meeting and couldn't make it for six o'clock. With an unlimited capacity for biting off more than I could chew, I offered to fill in on drums for the dinner music part of the evening, in spite of the fact that I had never played the drums in my life. Bryant would drop off his kit earlier in the day and I could tap along quietly to selections from shows expertly played by the proper musicians. Everyone talks during dinner anyway and nobody would really notice as long as I didn't try to large it up. Steve could avoid trying to get a drummer at short notice for the first part of the evening and everyone would be happy. After all I'd be wearing a dinner jacket and bow tie!

As the dinner wore on I grew in confidence and even executed a few syncopated fills using the brushes on the snare drum - but all very tasteful. This part of the evening would soon be over and we'd get a break while they were having toasts and speeches. Beer and sandwiches provided in the back room. Great! It was quite a posh do and a toast master, resplendent in a red coat had been booked to introduce the speeches and generally act as master of ceremonies. He came up to the mic, blew at it and said in stentorian tones "Ladies and
Gentlemen - The Queen…"

The rest of the band looked at me expectantly. Incapable of providing the required drum roll, way beyond my abilities, I did the only thing possible which was to lean down to fix an imaginary problem at floor level while Jimmy did a pub piano type rolling chord, a sort of 'glung a lung a lung a lung''. Eminently suitable for a number like 'My old man says follow the van' but totally inappropriate as an introduction to her Majesty's anthem. Everyone in the room stood up and sang God Save The Queen, for which I was at least able to provide a suitable crash on the cymbals at the end.

On another occasion the lovely Barbara Thompson was playing saxophone and had the audience's rapt attention throughout the evening until I suddenly realised that for some reason they were looking at me. It was then that I smelt burning and saw that my amplifier was on fire. Those were the days.

The BBC was formed on 18 October 1922 and started broadcasting from 2LO, Marconi's studio in the Strand, on November 14, 1922. Fifty years later in 1972 was the Jubilee year and various events marked the occasion. All members of staff received a set of commemorative stamps. I still have mine somewhere I think. Radio 1 producer Malcolm Brown and DJ Mike Harding wrote a song called Rocking At The BBC. Malcolm played piano, Mike Harding and Mike Franks played guitar. Fortunately this time Bryant Marriott was available to play drums and I was invited to play bass. DJ Pete Drummond was the vocalist. His wife Celia Humphrys, the only professional in the room, did backing vocals. We all turned up one night at Langham studio one, newly fitted with eight track tape facilities. We recorded three tracks that night, Rocking At The BBC, Goodbye and The Laughing Policeman for which song Malcolm patiently taught me the proper bass line. It was not the first time I had wished I had paid more attention to Miss Cobb's piano lessons and learnt to sight read music. It would not be the last. Somehow or other Warner records decided to release the song but we needed to re-record it. After this we were called in to do The Old Grey Whistle Test on BBC2 with presenter Bob Harris. This was recorded in a tiny studio at TV Centre and transmitted later on the same evening which allowed enough time to drive home and watch. It still exists somewhere on the internet.

During my time with pop music and light entertainment SMs (or POA's or studio engineers or whatever we were called at the time), there were a couple of excursions to make life even better. The first was a live outside broadcast from a ship leaving Liverpool with people emigrating to Canada. I was only a junior member of the team but I remember the production was complicated. It took a couple of days to rig all the gear with cables everywhere. The Northern Dance Orchestra played in the ship's ballroom and there were interviews with the ship's crew as well as people emigrating to Canada. To make it even more complicated the broadcast started as the ship sailed, so radio links to the shore were needed. The programme was then sent to Radio 2 continuity in London. The whole thing was handled by Manchester's outside broadcast engineers with a few operational staff from London.

When the show finished we had gone some way down the Mersey and the boat stopped. Next, literally nearly all hands on deck to de-rig the gear and load it into a tender which took us back to the port. The Northern Dance Orchestra had made for the duty free bar while this was going on and when the time came to depart there were one or two examples of unsteadiness when transferring to the tender. When you listen to these programmes at home they sound simple but the amount of effort needed to make them happen is huge, although for me at the time it was brilliant fun.

The second excursion was to the Belgian seaside resort of Knokke Le Zoute in Belgium. The event was a song contest organised by Nordring, a sort of club for broadcasters from countries around the North sea. Producer Jimmy Grant, presenter Brian Matthew and myself were the BBC's representatives. Our mission was to present Radio 2's Night Ride for a few evenings from Knokke Le Zoute. Jimmy and I arrived by car the day before the first broadcast whereupon all of our equipment was confiscated by the Belgian customs people. We got it back with the help of our hosts at Belgian Radio who provided most of the technical facilities. The programmes went out at 10 pm every evening and consisted of records, tapes of sessions made in London and interviews with performers at the song festival which took place in a grand casino on the seafront. We had the use of a makeshift studio in a couple of rooms with the usual glass window between the control room and the studio with Brian at the microphone. A local engineer acted as tape operator and I sat at the mixing desk controlling the sound levels. The broadcasters from the other countries were delightful and there was a party atmosphere for the whole week. My limited french was not needed for two reasons; a) because everyone spoke english and b) France was excluded from this exclusive club. I was with the A team and they made it look so easy. Brian Mathew already a legendary broadcaster had the most flawless technique I have ever seen and Jimmy Grant was prepared down to the last detail of every show. They had worked together on Saturday Club for many years and had nothing to prove. Junior as I was in every respect they made me feel like an equal which I most certainly was not. I think of it as a huge honour to have been able to work with them at that time.

This was before the days of mobile phones. Being abroad, even as close as Belgium seemed a long way away. Calling my girlfriend from the hotel would have cost an arm and a leg and so while setting up the transmission one evening I managed to get through via the control line for the broadcast only to find that she was out dumping a previous boyfriend! We were married a few months later and were together until she died in 2014. I still miss her.

Working in "Group A SMs" - pop music and light entertainment was a huge privilege, watching so many different types of performers creating radio shows. When John Peel went on holiday Vivian Stanshall of the Bonzo Dog Band stood in for him. I was junior SM on some of those sessions which in addition to the usual pre-recorded music were filled with sketches and jokes, hugely original stuff put together on the spot and using the studio as part of the creative process. Time consuming but brilliant.

He even enlisted the help of his friend Keith Moon to play drums and generally fool around, together with members of the Bonzo Dog Band.

Chapter 7: A trip to Maida Vale

One day in 1970 John Clarke who was our manager called me into his office. "You have to go on an advanced POA course." As you may imagine, I knew everything at the age of 23, so I didn't want to go. After a short discussion John left me in no doubt that I was going. That meeting changed my life. There were lectures on things like microphone placement, echo techniques and balancing music and drama. Good fun actually and sociable hours for a couple of weeks. One of the things on the course was a visit to the Radiophonic Workshop at BBC Maida Vale Studios.

The Maida Vale building was built in 1909 as a roller skating palace which claimed to be the largest in the world. The BBC took it over in the 1930s. It was home to the BBC Symphony orchestra in studio one and had four more studios recording music of all kinds and much later a state of the art drama studio built in the 70s. I was told that the design of this used new methods of sound insulation to combat noise entering from outside. Broadcasting House was due for a massive refurbishment and one of the problems was the Bakerloo line running beneath. There were frequent interruptions during drama recordings while a tube train passed. In the early years this went unnoticed because of the general background noise of early radio sets but when FM broadcasts came in, unwanted noises were a problem. Acting styles have changed too with more dynamic range, (some would say mumbling). Maida Vale six provided a prototype for these advanced methods of sound insulation. In 1980 I was lucky enough to be introduced to Rudy De Sylva, an architect working on the project. When he heard I was planning to build my own studio in a rented building he very kindly gave me no end of advice and help with the design within my limited budget.

But back to 1970. All the Maida Vale studios were at basement level. Radiophonic Workshop was at street level which must have been the original skating rink's balcony in earlier years. We had daylight from windows which looked onto the street but the sound insulation was poor because our 'studios' were really just offices. The film unit was based further along the corridor from the Workshop. They recorded the soundtracks of new movie releases for use in radio programmes. In earlier years when I was a studio manager I sometimes worked there recording soundtracks from the projector. Chitty Chitty Bang Bang comes to mind. They also recorded interviews with stars promoting their work. We often encountered well known faces in the corridor.

On a more sombre note they prepared obituaries for major stars so that they were instantly available for news broadcasts.

In 1977 Bing Crosby came to do a recording in studio three. It is said that a film unit producer saw him waiting at the reception desk, thought he looked unwell and updated his obituary. Sadly he died three days later on a golf course in Spain. There is a plaque on the wall of the studio where he made his last recording.

Before I joined the Workshop I had worked in the studios recording pop bands for Radios One and Two. At that time there were no multi track recorders or state of the art mixing desks. That came later when the refurbished studios gained legendary status for recording acts for John Peel's show and other programmes. Sad to say the building was sold recently and so at the time of writing it looks like we will be saying farewell to Maida Vale. I had done sessions there as a tape operator, but was unaware of Radiophonic Workshop apart from a vague idea that it was connected to Dr Who.

About twenty of us arrived at Maida Vale one afternoon and were directed along the long corridor on the ground floor to the "piano room" where we were given a talk by Desmond Briscoe, Organiser, Radiophonic Workshop. Malcolm Clarke was playing the taped examples, wearing his signature bow tie. Some of the lecturers on our course were less than engaging, particularly at three o' clock in the afternoon, but this was not the case with Desmond. His enthusiasm for the subject and the polished presentation kept us awake to the very end, when he invited us to get in touch if we were interested in doing a one week "attachment" to the workshop. The way things worked at the BBC in those days was that job vacancies were filled internally if possible. Notice boards everywhere had job adverts for available posts, anything from canteen staff to heads of department, film editors, production assistants and vision mixers. Many of those were for three month attachments which gave both the applicants and the department an opportunity to get a better idea about whether or not they would drive each other crazy. Then if a vacancy came up there was hopefully a pool of suitable applicants with experience to choose from.

The Radiophonic Workshop was a small department. Four "assistants" who did the creative work, a technical assistant, a maintenance engineer, a secretary and the organiser Desmond Briscoe. It would have been risky to have someone for a whole three month attachment if they didn't fit into the team, particularly as they would mostly be in close contact with the creatives who could be tricky... The solution was a one week trial before offering a three month attachment. The weekly 'attachees' were discussed at the dreaded mid monthly meeting and if liked they were invited back. I was very taken with the idea of combining music and technology so I did get in touch, which resulted in the offer of a one week attachment.

Desmond Briscoe worked as a studio manager in radio drama in the 1950s. He was interested in the work of early pioneers of electronic music in France and Germany. At that time tape machines were being installed in BBC radio studios making complex editing and manipulation possible. At the same time radio drama productions were exploring "things of the mind" - to quote Desmond - thus creating a need to develop sounds somewhere between conventional music and sound effects.

In 1957 productions of 'The Disagreeable Oyster' by Giles Cooper, 'All that Fall' by Samuel Becket and 'Private Dreams and Public Nightmares' by Frederick Bradnum all featured electronic effects made by Daphne Oram and Desmond Briscoe. They improvised facilities for making this material by assembling tape machines and other equipment in conventional studios at Broadcasting House while the studios were vacant, usually overnight. This encouraged BBC bosses to recognise the need for a permanent facility for producing electronic sound and in 1958 the Radiophonic Workshop was established in two rooms at the converted skating rink in Delaware road, Maida Vale studios. That sounds easy when you say it quickly but a lot of badgering would have taken place to make it happen. Desmond once remarked that persuading BBC management to do something was like fighting with a sponge. The unit consisted of Desmond and Daphne with engineers Richard Bird and Jean McDowell. Dick Mills joined six months later as an engineering replacement for Jean McDowell who left the Workshop at the same time as Daphne. The equipment at the workshop in those early days was gear that had been thrown out by other departments, "redundant plant". Installation and maintenance was carried out by Richard Bird and later by Dave Young who invented many innovative pieces of gear during the 60s and 70s. Dave once told me over a coffee in the canteen that one of the best days of his life was during the war when the Lancaster bomber he was occupying received a direct hit over Germany. Parachuting down over the Fatherland he felt a sense of relief, knowing that he was far more likely to see the end of the war alive in captivity than as a member of the bomber's crew. After being captured, as a prisoner of war he managed to clandestinely build radio sets from junk and a few parts supplied by a friendly german guard. What better training for inventing gadgets for electronic music making?

Daphne Oram left after about a year to work on a system she had devised called Oramics. Musical notes were generated by drawing waveforms onto film. She did this in a converted oast house in Kent. It was a ground breaking concept in many ways but sadly never really took off commercially. Desmond took over at that point as organiser of the department.

It seems hard to believe but in the early 50s radio was King, with only a small number of television viewers. The tide turned when a huge number of people bought TV sets to watch the coronation in 1953. By the end of the decade TV had the lion's share of evening audiences. Quatermass and the Pit was the first TV show undertaken by the Workshop in 1958. Desmond made electronic sounds for the TV sci fi series. This hugely popular show attracted far more attention than high-brow productions on the third programme and put the Workshop firmly on the map.

Over the next few years more creative staff were recruited. Delia Derbyshire had worked as a teacher and later in music publishing before joining the BBC as a studio manager. In 1962 she joined the Radiophonic Workshop. Brian Hodgson joined in the same year; he had been an actor in Rep before joining the BBC as a studio manager in radio drama. John Baker arrived a year later; he was a jazz pianist and had studied piano and composition at the Royal Academy Of Music before joining the BBC as a studio manager. Four years passed before David Cain arrived in 1967. He had a mathematics degree and was a jazz bass player. He previously worked as a drama studio manager in radio.

Other staff, usually studio managers, came to work for short periods, notably the talented Maddalena Fagandini who, among other things composed the interval signal "Timebeat". Television presentation in its early days was far less slick than it is now. Much of the output was live, there were very few studios and sometimes time was needed to change scenery or line up equipment. At these points there an interval perhaps filled with a still picture of a vase of flowers or a film of a potter's wheel. Maddalena's catchy electronic rhythm was used to accompany one of these interludes. In 1962 George Martin added instruments to her track and released it as a record under the name "Ray Cathode", months before the Beatles arrived at Abbey Road studios to make their first record.

On the first day of my one week attachment I reported to room 9 at BBC Maida Vale. I was shown into room 10 which at that time was used as a common room. Desmond Briscoe welcomed me and talked about the worksop's activities. At first he seemed like a typical BBC executive, I was in my 20s, he was in his 50s. He asked about my interests and I talked about my gigs playing guitar. The BBC exec. instantly changed into a drummer who had run a dance band in the 40s. And an enthusiast of using tape as a creative medium. He listened patiently to a short rhythmic piece I had made during spare moments in a recording channel.

He explained that it was not a 9 to 5 job. Work as long as you like, depending on what is going on, and take time off to make up for working longer hours. He suggested I might like to make a short piece using any free studio space before the end of the week. No pressure! It was now up to me to introduce myself to the creative staff and watch the proceedings or offer to help out, all very informal.

The idea was to watch what was going on and assist with editing or mixing while the assistants went about their work "realising" electronic music and sound. 'Trailing' was a common practice in the BBC - simply hanging around watching people working, a great way of learning. I had done loads of it as an operator, and sound balancer. Film editors vision mixers and many others learnt that way. Unfortunately it's not easy if you are writing music or experimenting with sound to have people watching over your shoulder. It's a self conscious process with lots of trial and error, frequent dead ends, bum notes, spectacular failures of taste and fumbling, before occasionally a wow moment happens. A bit like watching a conjurer practicing.

This resulted in people downing tools as soon as you arrived and simply chatting. Until you allowed them to get on with whatever it was they were doing and left the room to knock on someone else's door.

John Baker was working away in room 11 with his unique style of tape manipulation. He was polite and rather shy. Everything about the room was neat and orderly. Tape machines and a mixer. Tape loops of favourite sounds hung on hooks, a single piece of music manuscript paper in a neat hand rested on the desk. There was a shelf with a couple of exotic looking bottles which had provided the sounds for some of the the tape loops. And a wooden ruler, a chinagraph pencil and a plentiful supply of razor blades and sticky tape. No clutter of laboratory junk to be found later on in my tour. Not a cable out of place. Just an old electronic organ and an ashtray. We talked about the other people at the workshop, most of whom I was yet to meet. Then he showed me how he produced his unique style of music, tuneful and a bit jazzy, Cool and contemporary at that time.

The equipment was basic. A tape machine was modified to change speed in exact steps. A short tape loop of a pitched sound - say a cork popped from a bottle - was set up to play on this machine. Playing the loop at double the speed would produce a note one octave above. All the intervals in between were marked on a special switch calibrated in semi tones. John usually wrote his arrangements beforehand, sometimes on the commuter train from Southend on Sea. Having selected sounds for tune, bass line and accompaniment he set about copying the individual notes for each part onto a second machine running at the standard speed of fifteen inches per second. Now all the notes for each part were in order on a tape. After selecting a tempo it was a simple calculation to work out the length of tape required to produce a crotchet, quaver, semi quaver etc. If you want to take my word for it, skip the next paragraph!

For example at a tempo of 120 beats per minute in 4/4, each bar of music lasts 2 seconds. The length of tape of a bar at 15 inches per second is 30 inches. So the length of a crotchet is a quarter of 30; seven and a half inches.

Working from the score he was able to assemble the tunes by cutting notes of the correct length together using a ruler, an editing block and sticky tape. He would then play three tape machines in synchronisation and mix the elements together to produce the final result. This was a lengthy process and also involved careful mixing, equalisation, (tone control) and the addition of echo and reverberation. Much of the process was routine and believe it or not, he often had Radio 4 on in the background as he worked.

Many pieces of music were made by various people at the workshop using this technique but nobody matched John's skill at injecting musicality into this somewhat mechanical process. He was a jazz musician and understood the value of subtle variations of note lengths and volumes so that the piece sounded 'played' rather than mechanical. For me totally fascinating! But his tell tale glance at the clock prompted my exit to allow him to meet his deadline undisturbed.

No reply to my knock on the door to room 12. A bit early for Delia? OK, so on to room 13. The sound of sackbuts, crumhorns and recorders indicated that the room was occupied. The music stopped and as I entered a bearded and bespectacled dark haired man greeted me. He offered his hand and smiled in the slightly intimidating manner of a contestant from University Challenge.

David Cain had arrived in 1967. He had a mathematics degree, was a jazz bass player and had previously worked as a drama studio manager in radio. He was interested in using early musical instruments and sometimes blended them with electronic sounds. Some of his theme tunes appear on the album BBC Radiophonic Music originally released in1968. Later on he was engaged in blockbuster radio programmes supplying music and atmospheres, including The

Hobbit, The War of the Worlds, Isaac Asimov's Foundation Series and The Long March Of Everyman.

We chatted about his projects and found common ground in Jazz Club. I was usually second technician for the live Radio 2 show from the Playhouse theatre in Charing Cross on Wednesday evenings. David was enthusiastically into jazz. But the glance at the clock came in due course to signal the end of our meeting and I left to talk to the engineers in the maintenance room, Dave Young and Howard Tombs, followed by a chat with Dick Mills who was in room 10 typing out an article on fish in between shows, which caused an immediate misunderstanding. I imagined hooks, a trout stream and waders whereas Dick's passion which remains to this day was for aquarium fish. He has written many books and articles on the subject and is an expert in fish circles. Dick is and was then very easy to talk to and gave me an instant view of the new cast of characters in my life with disturbing honesty. A glance at the clock, lunch time! The canteen beckoned.

After lunch a visit to Room 12, the domain of Brian Hodgson and Delia Derbyshire. I was instantly welcomed and it was not long afterwards that I became a (junior) member of the team. But more later. I only have a vague memory of the rest of that week which ended with another chat with Desmond, playing the piece which I had spent some time making during the evenings. Would I be interested in returning for three months if invited?

Definitely yes please.

Chapter 8: The Workshop

Soon afterwards I went back for three months and got to know more about what was to be my workplace for the next ten years. I arrived as a single bloke sharing a flat in Shepherds Bush. When I left I was married with three children in a house called Honeysuckle Cottage in Woking. My bashed up Fender Telecaster guitar joined me at the workshop and over the next ten years contributed to much of the music I made.

At the start of the three month attachment the routine was to assist the creative staff, editing mixing, generally running around being useful and learning how it all worked. John Baker worked alone and seldom needed help. David Cain was generally the same at that time which left Delia and Brian who welcomed me into the room 12 club. I owe a great deal to their generosity of spirit. They often worked together and were great friends, supporting each other through the ups and downs of their personal lives.

Brian completely changed my somewhat bigoted attitude to gay people. This was 1970, only a short time since it had been illegal to have a homosexual relationship. It seems strange now but in general, attitudes then were totally different from today's. He told me about his situation because he wanted to reduce awkwardness when we worked together. His simple words live with me now - "It was not my choice - I would have chosen to be like you with, a girl who will be your wife and have children together".

He didn't open up to all the people at the workshop and he is one of my dearest friends to this day. I thank him for helping me understand at a time when, hard to believe now, so many of us were ignorant and intolerant. Delia's romantic life had its dramatic moments too and Brian was always there for her as she was (mostly), for him. It was such fun working with those two! I learnt tons of things technically and even more about the "mystique" side of things - there is a lot of snake oil salesmanship in Radiophonics! But above all they were aware of the possibility of creating magic. Not an exact science, but you know it when it happens. That's what you are always trying to get, often exploiting the 'happy accident'. How lucky to have had an apprenticeship with the best possible people.

They had worked with Peter Zinovieff in his studio in Putney, mainly on theatre projects, calling themselves Unit Delta Plus. Peter was more interested in researching computers and synthesisers and went on to form the synthesiser company EMS with David Cockerel, responsible for the VCS3, the first synthesiser to be used at the workshop and eventually the Synthi 100, christened the Delaware by the workshop. They later had a studio in Camden Town called Kaleidophon. Brian once jokingly called it "Catastraphon" But they did make an album called 'An Electric Storm', now a cult classic. David Voorhaus was the third member of the team behind this record.

The first show I was entrusted with on my own was 'A Highland Morning', a signature tune for Radio Scotland, no composing required but a version of a folk tune they had found - to be 'realised' on synthesised bagpipes. You could be forgiven for describing this as a poisoned chalice but listening to it all these years later it sounds ok. I was keen to get it right and the erratic tuning of the VCS3 was ideal for the job. A bit later Jeff Griffin asked me to make a theme tune and links for Scene And Heard, the Radio One magazine programme. With the aid of Bryant on drums and Nick playing bass we recorded backing tracks in Maida Vale studio 4 and I added the synthesiser tracks at the workshop. No multitrack machines so each extra instrument was added by copying the original tapes. I was still 'on attachment' at the time and I think that Jeff did me a huge favour by commissioning this because it demonstrated to Desmond that I could produce theme tunes. Thanks Jeff! And while we are on the subject, a few ex Radio 1 people occasionally meet up in a pub for a lunchtime rant about the BBC and at one of these gatherings I asked Jeff if he was going to write a book about his (amazing) career in production which includes among other things the In Concert shows for Radio 1. His reply was "No because I have been closely involved with a few top bands and I know that any publisher would want 'The Dirt'. The bands trusted me and I could not possibly betray that. The pressure would be huge so it's better to just say no". I very much admire this attitude in a world where few people care about these things.

Schools department in both radio and TV were good customers. The first show I did for them was in 1971 for 'Scene', a drama series made for teenagers which dealt with contemporary issues and intended to provoke discussion in the classroom. The episode was 'Just Love' written by Leonard Kingston and produced by Andrée Molyneux. When Desmond gave me the show I remember saying how appropriate it was for me. Lynda and I were getting married later that year. One of the tunes from that is on the Fourth Dimension album released in 1973. The next show for Andrée was 'Joe & The Sheep Rustlers' in the Look & Read series. This consisted of incidental music for the drama and songs to be sung by the cast. Once again Leonard Kingston was the writer. We were both surprised to be invited to visit the location for a day to watch the filming. Particularly as this took place near Todmorden in Yorkshire. This involved a pleasant train journey and a night in a hotel with visits to the filming locations in beautiful countryside. I am still not sure what the purpose of this was but it was great fun. Leonard had been an actor in the theatre and on TV before writing for the BBC Schools department. The train journey was a delight, for me at least. He was totally unassuming and full of amusing stories about his days in repertory theatre. We had in common the total inability to sell ourselves, even apologising for not being quite up to it. But he still went on to award winning success in his new writing career.

He was keen not to talk down to children and believed in portraying life as it was rather than sugar coating it. They would take what they felt comfortable with and ignore the rest, so within reason you could be much more adventurous than was usually thought acceptable. He proceeded to demonstrate the point with a story about his days touring in rep in the 50s. He was a stage manager at the time and the current production (somewhere out of town), was not getting enough laughs until a young Dora Bryan playing the part of a housemaid accidentally smashed an ornament while dusting somewhere in the background of a scene featuring the star Coral Browne as the lady of the house. The management liked this injection of humour and got them to repeat it in the next performance. By the time the show closed it had been expanded to become a lengthy tour de force with Coral Browne waiting 'patiently' in the foreground until the background antics came to a close with the line "Will there be anything further Madam? To which on one exasperated evening after the inevitable round of applause, the reply came " No… Now fuck off!" The performance continued after a brief pause and Leonard hurried to the bar at the end of the act to gauge the audience reaction to this shocking outburst. Not a single comment. The crowd must have assumed that they had simply misheard. After all, language of that sort was never ever allowed in performances in any medium in those days. So she couldn't have said it.

Words and Pictures was another TV Schools programme which I was involved with for many years, even after leaving the BBC. It all began when the talented graphic designer Liz Friedman asked me if I would do a theme tune for the show. She was making a new title sequence with animator Gil Potter. It was a wonderful show to work on with wacky cartoons and music to accompany stories based on children's books and songs. The producer Moira Gambleton was dedicated to the teaching values while insisting that the shows were engaging and entertaining. A whole generation enjoyed watching the programme while learning to read. The budget was small and so instead of hiring slick stage school kids (as heard in commercials) for the songs, Moira used local primary school children in exchange for a donation to the school. I made a backing tape which was sent to the music teacher so that the children were prepared in advance. One particular teacher insisted on involving all pupils including those who could not hold a note. Moira came up with a solution for this which was to listen in the studio and identify 'the groaners'. The 'choir' was then split into two groups each with its own microphone. One of the mics was not plugged in, which solved the problem with honour satisfied. On another occasion a version of 'Three Little Men In a Flying Saucer' was required. The teacher insisted on the children enunciating every single word, making it sound like something from nine lessons and carols. Some sort of compromise was eventually reached.

Moira helped a generation of children to read and many of them were inspired to love books by the programmes she made. The film editor working on that programme was Tony Kovaks, who had escaped from Hungary in the late 50s. He had worked in the film industry before coming to the BBC, notably as an assistant director on the film 'The Italian Job'. There were two crews one in Italy and the other in Ireland. Tony went to Ireland to film Noel Coward while another crew shot the famous car chase featuring minis coming down steps and driving through sewers. This brilliant sequence was much copied in commercials and of course became a lucrative source of work for those involved in the original filming. So Tony missed out on phone calls asking for 'the guys who made the car sequences for the Italian Job' and switched careers to become a film editor in the days when film was assembled on Steinbeck editing tables, physically cutting the shots together with 16 or 35 millimetre film. Video editing was very technically demanding in those days and only done by engineers. Tony eventually moved on to production and writing for BBC schools and later as a freelance even directed a film in the Cornish language. Tony is a shining example of why we welcome those who have escaped from tyranny to our fortunate shores.

When I first worked on Words And Pictures Henry Woolf was the presenter. He had been in the Doctor Who adventure 'The Sun Makers' for which I did the special sound. He played an evil alien tax collector. I imagine that suddenly seeing a favourite and gentle TV presenter transformed into a monster could have been a recipe for traumatising sensitive younger viewers! Vicky Ireland took over from him and I made music for many of the stories she narrated for the programme. She later ran the Polka children's theatre very successfully and I contributed music for some of her productions there. She wrote plays too and I have happy memories of working with her and her husband John Rowe who is a distinguished Radio actor.

The Workshop was not just a service department making material to order for producers. Encouraged by Desmond there was room to develop ideas for programmes made entirely in house. John Baker had a brother Richard who also worked at the BBC in news and current affairs. They were developing a radio programme together along the lines of the Jack Jackson show. For those under seventy I should explain that this was a series made by the legendary Jack Jackson in his own studio outside the BBC, with a mixture of records, links and slick wacky comedy clips. He paved the way for for a generation of DJs including Kenny Everett who said that he was the first person to have fun with radio. I think Richard was driving his brother John mad with his ideas and the whole thing was becoming a bit too much like hard work. John was not in robust health at that time and asked me if I would be interested in taking over, which I did. The programme was called Spinoff and began with a reverse tape effect; if you say 'fartnips and play the tape backwards you get something approaching "spinoff". The whole thing was done in odd bursts between other 'proper work' and was fun to do, driven by Richard's creativity and enthusiasm. He invented characters like the depressed DIY host Reg and created radio fantasies such as the dance band who went home leaving the dancers shuffling and humming. Fairly surreal. When the show was finally assembled we presented it To Simon Brett in light entertainment department who helped us to get it aired on Radio 2. It was a work in progress and Richard went on to much greater things as an editor of the Today programme and devising and presenting the obituary programme Brief Lives. Also writing books on the British musical including a biography of Marie Lloyd.

The question was always coming up. "Should we really be doing this? Is it really Radiophonic?" I made jingles for various local radio stations using singers, although the backings were synthesiser based. We all added session players to our work if budgets allowed. Was this proper electronic music? Producers had no doubts about using our services, sometimes because because it was much cheaper than hiring freelance musicians. But sometimes the answer to the question was a resounding yes, this really is 'Radiophonic'.

Doctor Who is an obvious example from the theme tune created by Ron Grainer and Delia Derbyshire to the special sounds of Brian Hodgson. Many jingles and theme tunes were not strictly speaking 'Radiophonic'. Were my jingles for BBC1's Christmas promos radiophonic? The answer is probably "No". The traditional tunes were played by trumpet and horns from the symphony orchestra. But a big part of the workshop's attraction was the ability to make things fit, do alterations and versions and give a one stop service. At that time getting a session organised with musicians in a conventional studio was not easy. The first discussions were largely about what you were not allowed to do because of Musicians Union rules. Then the composer was briefed and the session organised. At the end everyone went home and no alterations apart from a bit tape editing were possible. For many this worked well and the musicians and musical directors were staggeringly efficient and professional. But if there was a need for experimentation the workshop was sometimes more useful. Going back to the original question, "Should we really be doing this?" Of course Peter Howell's version of the Pizzicato from Sylvia arranged for a clucking chicken gets a resounding "Yes!", definitely radiophonic. And the imaginative sounds for 'Life Cycle' for schools radio produced by Arthur Vialls were totally Radiophonic. I was soon about to embark on a project where my contribution would be a hundred percent Radiophonic and without doubt what we 'ought to be doing'.

Chapter 9: Hitch Hiking

Simon Brett needed a few of sounds for a new radio series, including the end of the world. A quick glance at the BBC sound effects library in Western House revealed that this item was missing from its shelves. I had run into Simon a few times before, most recently with Richard Anthony Baker and so he knew that the workshop made weird noises to order. The pilot of the Hitch Hikers Guide to the Galaxy was about to be recorded at the Paris studio in Lower Regent Street (without an audience), and the plan was to bring the voice tapes to Maida Vale to put the show together in stereo and add the effects. Douglas Adams came too and was interested to see the setup at the workshop and be involved in the process.

Episode one mostly takes place on earth before its destruction by a Vogon spaceship so there aren't that many effects. I made the electronic sounds in advance working from the script. The code activating the book had a mixture of real sounds and synthesised bleeps cut together on tape. This was used throughout the various series. I made an alien voice treatment for the Vogon Captain as he addressed the people of earth over his p.a. system. The ship had a background hum and I borrowed the idea of sporadic bleeps from Startrek. That gave it a calm atmosphere. And of course the end of the world which I made up made up from explosions, train wrecks, animal groans and so on.

At the end of that session we went to the Warwick Castle a lovely pub near Little Venice, close to Warwick Road tube station. We sat outside with pints in the sun "The plan is .." said Douglas …"to get the pilot episode approved and then get the go ahead for a series" He wasn't a hundred per cent confident because this was the light entertainment (red nose) department of BBC radio. They mainly did shows with audiences and went in for getting big laughs. Hitch Hikers - at least episode one, because that was all that existed at the time, was a more gentle considered type of humour. The senior producers were old school comedy people and he wasn't sure they would get it. "The beauty of it is…" he said "that now the earth has has been destroyed we can go absolutely anywhere with it … If we can get it past the committee…"

Soon after that David Epps called me and asked if I would be interested in taking over his job as 'Music Producer further education' for three months while he was on attachment to another department. I initially said no because I had no musical qualifications whatsoever, not even a broad knowledge of the subject and this was Radio 3, real egghead stuff. He persuaded me, I think more out of a desire to get someone to fill in than from confidence in my abilities, although he knew I could put shows together. The series was to be called Music In Principle and the premise was that 'music has ingredients common to all styles. It is a mistake to listen to only one 'type' because there is much to appreciate in all of them if you take the time to listen'. David had set up some possible presenters, Philip Jones well known classical trumpet soloist, composer Bruce Cole, and concert Pianist Paul Roberts.

The programmes each had a theme common to all types of music, melody, harmony, film music, etc. I decided to split the half hour programmes into two parts, 20 minutes of chat about the topic, melody, harmony, rhythm, performance etc with musical examples. Then (at the threshold of boredom) an interview with various guests including John Dankworth, Phil Seaman and Jimmy Page. Not that the presenters were boring in any way at all! I had read somewhere that research had shown that for programmes requiring concentration, as opposed to background listening, people seem to need a change of gear after about twenty minutes.

Richard Rodney Bennet's theme was film music and after delivering his illustrated talk his guest was John Schlesinger, famous for directing Midnight Cowboy, Darling and many other films. He walked into the studio carrying a script which he put on the table saying to Richard "This is for you". An invitation to write the score for 'Yanks', his latest movie. That programme was delightful and easy to make but some of the others required more effort because some of the contributors were not professional presenters and took time to achieve a relaxed delivery. We even re-recorded one show much to the chagrin of that particular participant, but it had to be done.

Towards the end of my attachment to the department I needed one more show and after pursuing various dead ends decided to go for a sure fire winner. Steve Race was an utter professional and said he was too busy to do it when I first called him. I eventually persuaded him and he sent in a script which we recorded without any fuss in a short session. The title was "What a Performance". The Japan prize is a prestigious award for educational programmes and that programme won the Governor of Tokyo Metropolis Prize in the category of Adult Education. Steve sent me a note: "Humble piano thumper congratulates distinguished composer of PM theme tune on oriental award." He had previously been less than complimentary about my efforts in that direction.

Dudley Moore was one of those I was hoping would do a programme, a superb musician equally at home with classical and jazz. I phoned his agent who apologised because he wouldn't be available due to the fact that he would be flying to Los Angeles the following day to start shooting a movie. It was the year before his career in movies really took off with the release of 'Ten'. Obviously that was that. Until the following day, a Saturday when I was at home unblocking a drain and up to my armpits in mud when my wife Lynda came outside to tell me that Dudley Moore was on the phone. He was utterly charming and must have been in the middle of getting ready to fly off to the USA but had still taken the trouble to ring and say thank you and how much he would like to have taken part. He really didn't have to do that. I do so wish we could have made that programme.

By the time I returned to the workshop a few months later The Hitch Hikers Guide To The Galaxy was a big hit. Simon Brett and Douglas Adams had managed to get the pilot show past the committee and the first series was to be made. Simon had left the BBC to pursue his writing career and Geoffrey Perkins had taken over as the producer. The actors were recorded by Alick Hale-Munro and a team of studio managers at the Paris studio, located not in the Champs-Elisées but half way down lower Regent street. Dick Mills was assigned to provide the electronic effects, but after episode two Doctor Who intervened and so Harry Parker who was on a three month attachment to the workshop, took over that role. Douglas was very interested in the process and came to Maida Vale with Geoffrey Perkins for sessions to produce the effects and voice treatments. While Douglas and Harry were in room 10 wrestling with the Delaware synthesiser and the newly arrived Harmoniser to produce effects, Geoffrey spent idle moments perfecting his rendition of Lady Madonna in the piano room. This was typical of a good producer, allowing people to get on and work without constantly fussing around. Then see what they come up with and encourage changes if necessary.

In addition to the new digital harmoniser, traditional tape effects were used sometimes, such as sticky tape wound round the drive capstan of a tape machine to produce a wobble for Zarquon's voice.

Effective abuse of machinery. Slartibartfast, mice, the whale, Deep Thought, and Zaphod Beeblebrox all received loving attention to detail and sometimes robust discussion. Should Zaphod's two heads be panned left and right in the stereo picture?

Then the shows went back to the Paris studio for final assembly and mixing by Alick Hale-Munro with, over the series, John Whitehall, Colin Duff, Eric Young, Max Alcock, Martha Knight, Paul Hawden, Lisa Braun and Peter Harwood. They did brilliantly well and fulfilled Douglas's dream to create something more like a rock album than a radio comedy show. Geoffrey and Douglas were a great combination and I hope they wouldn't have minded me saying that the sum was much greater than the parts.

Pan Books released the book and I remember going to a launch party where everyone received a paperback copy which many people got Douglas to sign. Generous as always he had included a printed credit in the book for those of us who had worked on the radio series. I wish I had asked him to sign mine... the book sold in millions and was the beginning of his huge success story.

The next stage was the Christmas special and I was delighted to be asked to provide both sound effects and music for this show. Most of the music was to accompany the Peter Jones narrations and I tried to fit the music to his performance with changes of gear as subjects changed. There were comedy opportunities for effects, my favourite is the robot who blasts away the floor and falls to his death. After that an additional five programmes were recorded during 1979 and 1980. The BBC had decided it would be a fun idea to transmit the programmes over a single week rather than weekly episodes. 'They' didn't consider the huge strain for all involved. Douglas had not completed writing the material and as deadlines became impossible he was working on scripts in the studio and handing sheets to the cast as they went. Rock & Roll!

On the Monday of the transmission week only one episode was completed. We worked all hours to assemble the rest of the programmes. I had at least been able to do the music for all of Peter Jones's narrations which were recorded in advance. It's interesting that he never met the rest of the cast while working on the programme. By Friday sleep deprivation had set in and the last episode was completed in a daze. Later in the day Ann Ling, Geoffrey's assistant, had a friend lined up with a car to drive the tape of the final episode to Broadcasting house for transmission on Radio 4. We just about got it done by about six pm. Lisa Braun future wife of Geoffrey Perkins arrived to meet up with him together with the designated driver who was eager to grab the tape and get over to BH. But we had not had time to listen through to the programme to check if all the edits and retakes had been done. I hadn't been home for several days and divorce was threatened unless I made it back for a surprise birthday party that evening. "You go" said Geoffrey. Lisa was a studio manager and had worked on the shows. She would be able to do any editing needed. I left leaving them playing the tape while the ashen faced driver paced up and down the corridor outside. This story has been told before but if it is new to you, you may have guessed that there was indeed a retake left unedited. In modern speak, "My bad". Lisa was unfamiliar with the Studer tape machine and her nerve wracking attempt at cutting it out resulted in the machinery gobbling up some of the tape. Pressure. Fortunately all was resolved and snatching the tape box the driver ran down the corridor and drove off to BH, probably exceeding the speed limit.

There was a big audience that week and I was told that the figures for Radio 1 and Radio 4 were reversed as young people deserted their usual channel for the show.

Chapter 10: Rockoco

Meanwhile Richard Anthony Baker had introduced me to his actor friend Stephen Tate who was working on an idea for a rock musical called Rockoco with Jeffrey Shankley. At the time they were both in the musical 'A Chorus Line' in London's West End. They had performed or would eventually perform in all the top productions, Joseph, Jesus Christ Superstar, Cats, Starlight Express, etc.

Who better to create a new rock musical? They had written a few songs and I somehow got involved in putting together demo recordings. They could both sing, Jeff played piano and they had friends who would help out with extra vocals. The demos were good but the story line was rather vague and none of us had any idea where all this might be going. Then by a happy chance I was invited to a dinner in the council chamber at broadcasting house. The new managing director of BBC Radio, Aubrey Singer, held a series of events to which all radio producers were invited over a period of a few months. There were people from all departments, news, music, current affairs, drama, etc. The object was a general pep talk and an appeal for big blockbuster ideas. Overworked colleagues from production departments were slightly miffed by this suggestion - where would they find the time in their busy schedules to develop material like this? Encouraged by Desmond

Briscoe who was always keen on the idea of making complete productions at the workshop, rather than simply contributing music and effects to programmes made elsewhere in the BBC. I wrote a memo to the great man at broadcasting house suggesting that I may have the beginnings of the kind of thing he was looking for. He replied by inviting me to a meeting. Also present were Charles McLelland head of Radio 1 & 2 and assistant head Bryant Marriott. I did my pitch and played the tape of the songs which were generally well received but in fairness were fairly basic recordings. "How about a demo with a budget for musicians and singers to give a better idea of how a full production might sound?" Yes please!

When Stephen and Jeffrey arrived for our next session I revealed the news which unfortunately received a lukewarm welcome. Sadly Stephen was facing a personal dilemma and wanted to withdraw from the project. He generously handed his share to Jeff, wished us well and retired. All I can say is that I think the show would have been immensely better if that hadn't happened. But no use crying over spilt milk. I mentioned their contacts in the theatre world earlier and among those was the brilliant Anthony Bowles, arranger, conductor and hugely colourful character. Jeff and Steve had worked with him on various shows and wanted him to arrange their songs for choir and orchestra. He had been hugely involved with both Jesus Christ Superstar and Evita and ran the Superstar Choir, made up of singers from the shows on in London. This group met at weekends to sing together. It is a measure of the high regard they had for Anthony that after a hard week performing in the West End they found the time to do this. He was a perfectionist and could be tough when things were not right but they adored him and gave their best.

We went to see him at his house in Islington and had tea in the kitchen. We explained what it was all about and played the tapes of the songs. We wanted him to arrange them for a small band and choir to provide a demo for the BBC bigwigs. We had been given a small budget for this and if it went well we could be making the show for Radio 2. He was (rightly) highly sceptical of whatever I might have to contribute but looking at it now I can see that he saw it as a way of giving much needed work to lots of people rather than an opportunity for himself. He agreed to do the demo and the next time we met was at Maida Vale studio 4 on a Sunday afternoon. He had asked to be free in the morning to serve at his church in Hampstead. His faith and commitment to others were both important in his life. I admired that as much as his amazing talent.

His arrangement of the songs for the small band of musicians plus lots of singers was great. Studio Manager Peter Watts brought the whole thing to life in lovely stereophonic sound. All of the musicians and singers were people Anthony had worked with in the theatre and they gave a hundred per cent to this talented leader. I wish I could convey his voice onto this page but suffice it to say that it was as camp as a row of tents. "Do you know the meaning of *'Andante'* Jeffrey?…" or "Loud, confident….. but unfortunately wrong, Jeffrey…"

We played the finished tape to the top brass and they liked it enough to ask how much it would cost to make the final product. A medium sized orchestra and chorus for a few sessions plus the soloists was not not cheap. We worked out the number of musicians, singers and sessions we thought were needed and did the sums with the help of the ladies in BBC contracts department who immediately put me in my place. "You do not discuss money with the artistes. At all… Ever…." We submitted the figures to the management and the answer came back with a touch of Déjà vu, "Yes. But can it be ready by 27th August?" Oh God! The pressure was on. Casting, full arrangements, and completion of the book…

It was a revelation to work with top performers from the world of musical theatre. Colm Wilkinson played the hero of the piece and was superb. The choir sounded great, drilled by Anthony Bowles who arranged the music and conducted the orchestra of session musicians. My role was producer, not composer or writer and I have learnt two things about production over the years.

(a) Book the best people for the job and then leave them to it.

(b) *But* listen to the small nagging voice in your mind when it tells you something is wrong. The first point was OK, all the best people were on board. I fell down on the second. Rockoco was a good idea with nice songs but not much of a story. I never managed to get that put right and fell into the 'it'll be alright on the night' syndrome. We should have got the book sorted out but suddenly we were in production and busking the storyline. If I had my time again I would approach it differently. We dished up something that sounded a bit like the West end shows of the day. But we should have made an adventurous piece with an engaging story, with the accent on rock rather than orchestral and featuring tons of Radiophonic effects. But there you go, we did what we did and the piece didn't go on to better things. Oh, except that it became the BBC's entry for the ultra prestigious Italia prize that year, an achievement not to be ignored. But it didn't win. Geoffrey Perkins listened to the show and commented "It *sounded* great"… But where was the story?" Hitting the nail on the head. I can only say " It seemed like a good idea at the time."

An invitation arrived from New York to a creative radio seminar organised by producer Larry Josephson. Somehow or other Geoffrey Perkins fixed it up for us to attend and talk about the Hitchhikers Guide which had become popular in the USA. It took place in a conference centre in Long Island and it was a surreal experience to discover that quite a few people had heard the show and liked it. When we gave our talk it was being beamed by satellite to other parts of the states. Amazing in the late 1970s. Larry Josephson had a radio show on WBAI-FM and he interviewed us for his programme one evening. There was time to go into Manhattan before returning home. We went to 48th Street Photo, a cut price electronics shop and Geoffrey bought a Sony Walkman. I got a Casio VL Tone, don't know why but I still have it. And I also went to a Broadway show, 'The Suspended Lightbulb' by Woody Allen.

Chapter 11: The Sequence

John Muir was Radio 1 producer working among other things on the 'strip shows'. Don't get the wrong idea, the strip programmes were devised to make typing out scripts easy, before the days of computers. Rightly or wrongly Radio 1 had a play list for the daytime shows, records chosen by a committee of production staff. Strips of paper were typed up for each record with all the information about the record including extra details not needed by the DJs but essential for reporting copyright information. These strips could be assembled in any order to make up a page which was photocopied. There were strips for the other items like jingles, the news and so on. This saved hours of repetitive typing. For a junior producer it was not massively creative to work on these shows. The DJs had their styles and day to day shows were made to a formula. All that was needed was to put the records in a suitable order, watch the timings and not put 'Fly me to the Moon' next to the news - in case of a plane crash.

Those producers wanted to devise their own programmes with more of their own creative input. John produced jazz shows which allowed him the choice of artists and he also devised 'The Sequence' which was a late night show once a week, part of 'Sounds Of The Seventies' The idea was to link the records with a dead pan back announcement after each record from DJ Pete Drummond accompanied by a short piece of specially recorded music to link the tracks. The budget allowed one or two musicians plus, guess who, a radiophonic person who was effectively free of charge. A three hour session in Langham studio one was used to record these links which were totally improvised. The musicians varied, Bob Downes, Manfred Mann, Stan Tracy, Brian Eno, Tony Ashton, Barry Guy, Ron Geesin and others. Plus me. I took along a guitar and a portable EMS synthesiser with a keyboard.

They played us the end of each record and a gap followed by the beginning of the next one and we did a link with a key change so that everything flowed. Pete Drummond's dead pan announcement was dubbed over the top of this. There was a lot to do in the time available; we had to establish the keys of the two tracks, come up with a mood, do a quick run through and then a take. With synthesisers we had to make the sounds too, there were no presets with the touch of a button to change the sounds.

I'm pleased to say I wasn't the only one to feel whacked at the end of these sessions, there were so many different items to do. The team in the control room was John Muir, Bill Aitken, and Maggie Garrard (later Rodford). We provided the raw material and they added echo and other effects to make it all blend together, and do a tasteful mix.

When Pete went on holiday John Muir managed to persuade Vincent Price to do the announcements.

He did it in splendid Hollywood horror style. The already surreal show took a step further into weirdness. The Sequence was an experiment and not unpopular at the time but the format has not been repeated which leads me to think that people really prefer some banter or bits of informed information. But it was huge fun for us at the time.

Working on it with John Muir and jazz saxophonist Bob Downes led me to Lily Greenham. The workshop had a history of working with experimental sound poetry and had made contributions to programmes with Ernst Yandl and Bob Cobbing. Lily had been married to freelance percussionist Peter Greenham and had a few mutual friends in the BBC symphony orchestra. She wanted to make a programme of 'Lingual Music' for BBC Radio 3. Desmond asked for volunteers to work on this experimental poetry show. I stood still and the others took a step backwards. This led to spending one day a week working with Lily on her sound poems, which was an unexpected pleasure because she was a delight to work with; making tape loops of her voice, cutting up vocal sounds and adding electronic sounds from the Delaware, a huge synthesiser newly arrived at the workshop. The man behind this project was George Macbeth, producer of poetry programmes for Radio 3 and a poet in his own right. He simply left us alone for several weeks to make the material.

One day George arrived to listen to to what we had produced. We were expecting suggestions for changes, perhaps rejection of some items and requests for new ones. He listened attentively to each piece making no comments but jotting down copious notes. After the last piece he said "Right, let's put the show together, where can we record the links?" He then recorded his voice linking the poems together to make a half hour programme. A bit of editing but all done before lunch. Compared to the tortuous processes employed by some producers this was a dream. The show was soon transmitted on Radio 3 without alteration.

Lily was a true artist with an independent spirit, she lived in a tiny room in north London. My wife Lynda and I were invited for a meal one evening and were amazed at the way she produced delicious food with only a one ring camping stove and minimal equipment. She went on to work with Desmond Briscoe and Peter Howell on a piece called Relativity for Radio 3. I think it may have won prizes.

I later did a few sessions with another colourful character Lady June. "Everything is Nothing" was the title of this dreamlike piece of sound poetry. One feature of June's daily routine was that she was unable to get to the workshop until after lunch when the effects of funny cigarettes had worn off. There was a brief respite until a new batch kicked in so it was essential to work fast.

I believe her album "Linguistic Leprosy" is still available.

I mentioned Harry Parker's contribution to the Hitch Hiker's Guide earlier on. He worked on other things as well during his time at the workshop, including SOS with Barry Bermange who had produced Inventions For Radio with Delia. He and I made a radio show called "It Was In Tune When I Bought It", which was about how guitars had become popular in the late fifties. The title referred to a customer who had taken his guitar back to the music shop to complain that it was out of tune. We interviewed Hank Marvin at Maida Vale and he demonstrated his techniques with various guitars and effects. Harry went to see Pete Townsend and came back with an interview and demonstrations. What a dream to be able to meet the heroes of our teenage years. We had intended to include interviews with Bert Weedon, guitarist and author of "Play In A Day" and Jim Burns the famous guitar designer but decided to feature them at a later date because there was easily enough material for two shows. It never happened because both Harry and I moved on, so maybe we should revisit that one day. Harry went on to a successful career as a Radio 4 producer. Gillian Reynolds gave the show a nice review, describing how it evoked life during those early days of rock 'n roll. It is so wonderful when a listener, particularly an eminent reviewer "gets it".

The Saga of the Hitch Hikers Guide continued with the TV version. Once again a pilot was made before the producer Alan JW Bell got the go-ahead to make the series. He came to the workshop with sound supervisor Mike McCarthy to talk about the soundtrack. Rob Lord provided the graphics which accompanied

Peter Jone's readings. The computer animation effect was actually achieved using film techniques and cell animation, not a computer in sight. I first made the music to fit Peter Jones's narration with changes of key to point up subject changes. I was supplied with a sixteen millimetre film of the graphics and the next stage was to cut the bleeps for the words printing out on the screen using magnetic film so that they fitted exactly. When there was a key change I used bleeps matching the pitch. Some of the electronic sound effects were from the radio show but I mostly made new ones to fit the action on the screen. For example the sounds for the improbability drive section in episode three were made from scratch. Stephen Moore came to the workshop one evening to record all the Marvin voice parts which were added after the visuals had been shot. All very labour intensive! But it was liberating to be making both the effects and the music because conflicts between the two, so often a problem, could be avoided. It was hard work keeping up with the schedule but I still remember the buzz of putting together the end of the last episode. Emotional at the end of a project and trying to transition seamlessly into the final Louis Armstrong track. The organ in Maida Vale studio one produced the final chord in that episode which accompanied the producers credit. It took three people to get the maximum keys and pedals pressed. Kevin Davis who had worked with Rob Lord on the graphics was putting together a "making of" video and came to film the producer and me one afternoon. I believe that video is still around.

Douglas was keen to have control over his creation as all writers do but it is very difficult to achieve. Sometimes it's less painful to sign the contract and let go. It was a Light Entertainment department production and there were inevitably going to be conflicting ideas about the show. For example there was a session where an audience was dubbed onto the soundtrack. It simply wasn't that sort of show and thankfully the idea was abandoned. It is said when comparing Radio and Television that Radio has best pictures. Many fans of the radio version preferred it to the TV and I know the TV Marvin is certainly not how I imagined him visually. I suppose everyone would have a different idea which makes it very hard to get it right. Perhaps it's better to transfer a successful TV show to Radio rather than the other way round. Dad's Army worked because the characters were already well established visually. There was a second TV series of Hitch hikers planned but Douglas pulled the plug on that. I suppose the enormous success of the books gave him the financial freedom to make that decision which would have been hard for most writers. Most people will remember Douglas as a talented writer but I often think how generous hearted he was. When his first book, published by Pan became a huge hit he invited everyone including me and the team of radio studio managers, Geoffrey, production secretary - and the designated driver - to a slap up meal at the

Waterside Inn at Bray to celebrate. And we were picked up and returned in chauffeur driven limos. And a few years later Geoffrey told me that when he and Lisa suffered the tragedy of a cot death Douglas came to them immediately and stayed, taking over the housework, making tea, generally, comforting and was just there for them. That is real friendship. Very sadly both Douglas and Geoffrey died young.

Chapter 12: The Doctor

I am amazed by the number of people who are still passionate about the Doctor Who series from the 70s and 80s. Perhaps it's a good thing we didn't know that while we were making music and sounds or we would have frozen in panic! When I started at the workshop the show had been running for over seven years and the current Doctor was Jon Pertwee. Brian Hodgson made the special sound effects for each episode as well as drawing on the well loved standard sounds he had previously created, like the TARDIS and the sonic screwdriver. Room 12 had shelves containing tapes of all the sounds since the show began in 1963, all meticulously catalogued. Various composers were hired to write the music over the next few years including Richard Rodney Bennett, Carey Blyton, Tristram Cary, Francis Chagrin, Barry Gray, Malcolm Lockyer, Norman Kay, Don Harper, Stanley Myers, Harry Rabinowitz, and Humphrey Searle. Some of them came to the workshop either to add electronic sounds to an existing score or record the whole thing using synthesisers with Brian Hodgson or later on Dick Mills.

Dudley Simpson wrote the music for nearly 300 episodes starting in 1964. He was an experienced conductor in the theatre world and had been Margot Fontaine's musical director on tour. He used to joke that he was hired because he was the only person who could get the Perth symphony orchestra to sound OK. He also knew how to deal with temperamental stars - "Dudley this is too fast!" or "Dudley this is too slow!" "No Problem!" he would reply while, out of the corner of his mouth, - "Same tempo fellas."

He was flavour of the month for BBC producers and in addition to his Doctor Who scores he wrote music and theme tunes for many other shows including Moonstrike, The Brothers, The Ascent of Man, Moonbase 3, and Blake's 7. At one stage he was doing scores for all episodes Doctor Who and Blake Seven, a massive amount of work. He was a delightful man to work with and like many of the best people there was no "side" to him so that it was sometimes easy to underestimate the huge talent behind his straightforward exterior. The routine at that time was to record a small band of musicians at TV centre onto an 8 track tape which was then taken to the workshop where he and Brian would add sounds from the Synthi 100 machine and create a music mix to be dubbed onto the final programme back at TV centre. The combination of orchestral and electronic sounds was a winning formula at that time which was why Dudley was in such demand for sci fi shows. It must have come as a huge shock when one day in 1980 the new executive producer of Doctor Who John Nathan Turner invited him to lunch. Instead of discussing the next series, Dudley was told that his services would would no longer be required. I learned later that he was devastated by this. However he had had a wonderful run and those shows are still being watched all over the world today. The background to this is that John Nathan Turner had become the new executive producer of Doctor Who. He had previously worked on Drama series including All Creatures Great And Small. As a 'new broom' he wanted to update the look and sound of the show. Brian Hodgson had always thought that the Workshop composers ought to write incidental music for it, particularly in view of Delia Derbyshire's hugely successful work on the theme tune. After some discussion it was decided that Peter Howell and I would each do a section of music for an existing episode to demonstrate what could be done. I wish I still had that tape! To our delight the ideas were accepted and we began providing the incidental music for the series.

I have often wondered how Delia would have approached it. The problem was that the production had to be a bit of a sausage machine to make the amount of shows in the time available. Deadlines were tight and the music had to be on time and fit the picture. The use of synthesisers made all this possible whereas with the old methods it would have taken far too long to produce the goods. By the time the opportunity arose Delia had left the BBC. But with the right approach I think it could have been done. When we first worked on the shows we were locked in to the methods they had used for years, scoring to picture. Looking back I think we may have sometimes made everything fit a bit too well, "Mickey Mousing" the action.

I believe Delia could have made a library of material in advance and then worked with a music editor to fit sections to the visuals. We will never know but I can say that before all this when she was in her prime Delia would have loved doing some of the incidental music for Doctor Who.

I was lucky enough to have a go at a time when synthesisers and multitrack tape machines were around which made the process of being a one man band much faster. Not so with the early EMS synthesisers which were complex sound sources not really designed for producing conventional music, unlike the newer models from Arp, Roland and Oberheim which were much easier to use. On Tuesday June 10th 1980 I went to Threshold house on Shepherds Bush Green to look at my first episode in one of the Dr Who offices. Those present at the Review were director Peter Grimwade, his assistant and Dick Mills who would be making the special sound effects. We watched a VHS tape of the episode which had a clock superimposed at the bottom of the picture.

It has been said that the most important decision to make when writing music to picture is where you have it and where you leave it out. Some directors had mastered this art and knew how to place cues most effectively and where to leave silence or play the scene on sound effects. In general when using electronic music mixed with electronically produced sound effects, unpleasant clashes can occur. For example if the spaceship has a background hum it is almost impossible to combine that with a music cue. So the trick is to mix the sound so that one or other is featured. This did not always happen and so the decision at this early stage to use music where natural sound was present and leave it out where electronic effects were present was usually a good one.

It's also important to ask the question what is the music doing here? It is useful as a link between scenes or to indicate the passage of time. It can provide an atmosphere of unease or danger. Or gradually build tension. Or suggest all manner of things from romance to 'don't trust this person', or (frequently in Doctor Who), the presence of pure evil. Music seems to be able to convey things words can't and when writing it the unconscious mind is good at coming up with tunes that say things. Sadly we were often asked (not just in Doctor Who), to 'paper over the cracks' when something hadn't quite worked out - a diversion in a less than perfect scene. We were experimenting with technique; it was sometimes fun to end a music cue abruptly just before a line of dialogue which gave that line more weight rather than the expected line, a bit like putting the spotlight on the supporting actor. However these experiments rarely made it into the final versions. But no such thoughts for this my very first episode. Leaving the building clutching scribbled notes and a VHS tape I returned to Maida Vale to start work that afternoon.

Only a short time before that Dudley Simpson did not have the luxury of taking home a video tape.

He took away notes of timings and then wrote most of his music to a click track, a metronome beat at 120 beats per minute which made hitting picture cues (synch points) relatively easy. He was skilled at writing 'across the beat' which gave the impression that the music did not sound as if it was all at one tempo.

We devised a different approach. A voice counting track was produced counting minutes and seconds from nought to thirty minutes. For a given music cue a bleep was placed at all the timings where some event was required. It was then possible to make a metronome track of any tempo to lay against this template and write out a bar sheet with all the synch points marked.

Unlike the film industry we did not have the means to record our music while simultaneously watching the picture, something which is taken for granted now even in the most modest bedroom studios. As I said before we may have sometimes been aiming at making the music fit rather too much. It's much more effective sometimes to produce an atmosphere which fits the mood of the piece without continually emphasising moments in the action. To quote the great Henry Mancini "Everything fits Everything". You can try this at home. Play any piece of film with the sound tuned down. Now play any piece of music and see how well it fits the picture cuts. The mood may be wrong but the actual fitting usually works well. That's partly because film editors have a rhythmic feel to their cutting even when there is no music in a sequence.

Fortunately I had done special sound for Doctor Who for The Sun Makers in 1977, so I was not completely unfamiliar with the production routine. For that series I had tried to adopt a more organic approach to the sound effects rather than using entirely electronic synthesiser based sounds because I was aware aware of the frequent clashes between music and effects.

The final sound dub took place in a room at TV centre called the Sypher suite; SYnchronised Post-dub Helical-scan and Eight track Recorders. That is as technical as this is going to get. It's enough to say that all the final elements of the sound track, dialogue, sound effects, and music were assembled and mixed to the final soundtrack to be heard by the viewer at home. Present were the director, sound supervisor, tape operator, Dick Mills, (special sounds), and the music composer. Naturally everyone thinks that their contribution is most important and that it should be louder in the mix than the others and the sound supervisors were often driven mad by arguments about the sound balance. At the end of the day the show was reviewed and executive producer John Nathan Turner came along to give the thumbs up or ask for changes.

I feel so fortunate to have been involved in the programmes and humbled when people compliment my contributions. The end of Logopolis is a well remembered sequence where Tom Baker transforms into Peter Davidson. An emotional moment which I was privileged to accompany. I did the music for five series each with four episodes at the Workshop. Full

Circle and Logopolis directed by Peter Grimwade, State of Decay and The Visitation for Peter Moffatt and Castrovalva with Fiona Cumming.

Two more adventures were to follow after leaving the BBC, Mawdryn Undead for Peter Moffatt and Frontios for Ron Jones. I didn't know how lucky I was at the time and looking through my old diaries I see that each episode took under a week including the review and the sound dub.

For some reason many viewers who watched the programmes as children who are now in their 40s and 50s still have huge affection for the amazing Doctor Who.

Chapter 13 People

Here are the people I was privileged to work alongside at the Radiophonic Workshop. We seldom worked together because we each had our own projects. Desmond Briscoe once said "You can have all the equipment in the world but without the right people you won't create a note of music". Actually he said it quite a few times in his lectures and demonstrations. He was at heart a performer and loved appearing in public talking about the workshop, of which he was rightly proud. In the fifties and sixties Large exhibitions were popular and mostly took place at Earles Court or Olympia. The Ideal Home Show, The Motor Show, The Boat Show, etc. He appeared on the BBC stand at the Radio Show at Earls Court. He introduced items including the sounds he had made for early radio dramas and TV's Quatermass and the pit. Also demonstrations of how sound could be manipulated with echo, pitch change and so on. This grand production led to a string of smaller engagements around the country, speaking at clubs and after dinner events.

I was involved in one appearance in 1971 which took place at the Festival Hall on the south bank. The Institute of Electrical Engineers were celebrating their centenary which was attended by Her Majesty the Queen. When Desmond gave his presentation Malcolm

Clarke and I were with him on the stage playing the examples from tape machines. There were slides too and Dick Mills was in charge of a projector in the front row of the otherwise unoccupied circle. When the Queen rose to leave, the audience in the stalls were on their feet applauding enthusiastically and she replied with a suitably regal wave. Turning to the circle she found that the only occupant was Dick with his slide projector, but gave him a special wave anyway.

Thinking about it now I realise that Desmond was much more in touch with the listeners and viewers than many BBC executives because he actually went out and engaged with people. Doctor Who was a bit of a double edged sword for him. Wherever he went, at the mention of Radiophonic Workshop the standard reaction was "Oh Doctor Who!" - as if that was the only thing they had done. Of course when a large credit appears every Saturday announcing the name to millions of people on national TV, what do you expect? And to a degree he was responsible for that by energetically promoting the workshop and insisting on proper credits being given at the end of programmes. In those days of course it was still possible to read the credits at the end of shows whereas now in these competitive times they are reduced in size to accommodate promos for other shows.

As head of department or "Organiser" as he was known, Desmond definitely had the T shirt. He had been a studio manager in Radio Drama and later created electronic sound for the avant guard productions of the late fifties. He had an early hit on television with Quatermass and the Pit and so was no stranger to the popular end of the market. He was intensely practical in an area constantly requiring improvisation. The war had prevented him from going through university although he did later get a degree from part time study. His hobby was boating, about which he was passionate. Nothing on earth can compete with boats in preparing you for the unexpected! He lived by the Thames and had a mooring at the bottom of the garden. Once a year the Radiophonic picnic was held there and we were treated to joyrides in his canal boat Samanda (whose previous owner was Frank Muir.) His wife Gwyn was a teacher so Desmond saved up his leave to take extended summer voyages on the boat. His love of canals led to his production of an album for BBC records in 1969, Narrow Boats; Voices, Sounds and Songs of the Canals.

He was a strong and sensitive leader and had a clear idea of how this extraordinary collection of creative people should be run. He did away with set hours. Come and go as you please, day or night, as long as the work is done that's all that matters. If you work extra time at weekends or nights, take a day off to make up for it. He was extremely clear on how to present the finished work. Never ever send off a tape to a producer. Get the producer to come to the workshop and play the material in context while he or she is fully concentrating. There had been instances of music played at the wrong speed, even backwards or at a meeting with other things going on, and rejected for all the wrong reasons. People love to appear clever at meetings. Play it at the correct volume so that it is not intrusive; electronic sound was novel in those days and apt to annoy if it was too loud or played out of context. He encouraged freedom of expression and originality. Freedom to fail is a liberating experience.

Above all Desmond was sensitive to the problems of staff working under pressure and very supportive. He has sometimes been portrayed (by people who weren't there), as a sort of impatient bureaucrat but he wasn't like that at all. He must have spent hours listening to the problems of people going through a bad patch and in my experience was always sympathetic and helpful. But the individuals in any department are competing with each other however polite the facade. For small departments this is hard to deal with and Desmond had a delicate balancing act on his hands. When a new show came in he liked to allocate it to a composer as quickly as possible to avoid arguments. Peter Howell once described this procedure as 'Desmond walking down the corridor carrying a hot potato'. Of course there were disagreements at times. That happens when people care about their work. I remember Desmond raising his voice to Dick - "Why is it that when I ask you something you always reply with a question?" Dick replied "Do I?..."

In later years he made programmes with huge amounts of painstaking editing and mixing such as 'Relativity' which featured sound poet Lily Greenham and 'A Wall Walks Slowly' based on the poetry of Norman Nicholson. I remember Geoffrey Perkins and I were trying to arrange time in room 13 for a pressing deadline. The studio had been booked for days on end for one of Desmond's blockbuster shows. Geoffrey said "Hmm, a man produces slowly…" I'm glad to say that Desmond was affable and gave us our time in the studio.

Desmond retired from the BBC in 1983. He died in 2006 and his Humanist funeral took place in a crematorium. At the end of the ceremony Brian Hodgson said the words "Wherever his journey takes him in time and space we wish him well". His coffin went through the curtains to the sound of Doctor Who's TARDIS taking off.

Dick Mills was known as the workshop's oldest inhabitant. He arrived in 1958 to provide technical assistance to the creative staff. He later helped Delia with the legendary Doctor Who theme tune and spent many years making the special sound for that show after Brian left the BBC. He received an honorary doctorate from the university of Bradford in recognition of his achievements in that direction. He has since enthusiastically given presentations about his work. Of course he worked on many shows apart from Doctor Who over the years and provided sound for most of the legendary radio drama producers of the sixties, Charles Le Faux, Michael Mason, Hallam Tennyson, and John Tydeman, to mention just a few, who returned again and again for his work which was produced without fuss or unnecessary mystique. I remember he was asked to help with a Panorama programme. They got in touch late on a Friday asking for a huge amount of material for a programme to be transmitted the following Monday. They had obtained the rights to use film shot by Nasa in space. Stunning visuals but sadly no sound. They needed this missing ingredient and fast. Dick worked over the weekend to produce appropriate effects for the pictures. One of the production staff rang after the transmission with profuse thanks for a job well done and asked how the space craft sounds were made. Without a trace of pretentiousness Dick replied "Oh the old vacuum cleaner tape played backwards always comes in handy". Desmond was horrified by this lack of … 'mystique', (if that is the word).

Dick also worked on Dudley Simpson's music sessions for Doctor Who. Dudley scored his music for a small orchestra recorded at TMS, the TV music studio at Lime Grove and brought the eight track tape to the workshop to add electronic sound and do a final mix. That system began with Brian Hodgson and when he left the BBC it continued with Dick. I mentioned earlier filling in for an adventure called 'The Sun Makers' when Dick was on holiday. The Delaware synthesiser which took up most of room 10 had lots of oscillators which Dudley liked to tune to a chord to add weird textures to the orchestra. This was in the days before we had truly polyphonic synthesisers. Dick and Dudley must have spent many hours together on the Who sessions. Each episode required a briefing meeting with the director, a day at the workshop to add the electronic sound and a dub where all of the sound for the show was put together at TV centre. Dialogue, conventional sound effects like wind, motor cars and footsteps etc, Dick's electronic sounds such as guns, backgrounds, Tardis etc, and Dudley's music. This needed to be crammed into a track which would sound OK coming out of a tiny loudspeaker in a TV set. This was not an enviable job for the sound supervisor because all the participants were keen to feature their own contributions prominently. The committee usually struggled to a conclusion, hopefully without a punch up, at about the same time as the BBC Club bar opened to provide urgent refreshments.

Delia Derbyshire had a real presence and at first glance a slightly haughty manner. In fact she was quite shy and absolutely delightful when you got to know her. She had somehow lost her midlands accent at Cambridge university and when I first met her she was drinking a bit too much cheap wine and also taking snuff. I can't talk because I was smoking far too much at that time. The new EMS synthesisers were appearing then and both Delia and Brian had bought VCS3s for their private studio, Kaleidophon in Camden Town. Brian was much more taken with this new approach than Delia. It is a shame that it seemed that this new exciting technology spelt the end for the older methods like tape manipulation. Although this wasn't true at all, as it turned out, it did nothing for Delia's self confidence as the new machines started to appear at the workshop. It always happens, someone invents a saxophone or accordion and in no time at all there are whole orchestras of these new wonders until things settle down. But it was just one element of Delia's withdrawal from the front line. New keen young people arriving probably didn't help and one of those in particular had a negative effect on her. Delia always had a problem getting started on projects - we all do - but this got worse as time passed and many of us tried to help her. New versions of existing theme tunes is an example. Blue Peter wanted a new version of theirs, a sort of hornpipe played by an orchestra. The sheet music arrived from the music library and Delia set about working out how to approach it. I acted as an assistant and was delegated to help with getting sounds out of the newly arrived VCS3 while desperately attempting to keep it in tune, plus mixing the tracks. With Delia it would never be a collaboration and rightly so. I'm not sure how often it was actually used but it was not really a roaring success. The original version says it all and a sort of electronic barrel organ version doesn't improve on it. However I wish that they had asked Delia to compose a completely new theme for the programme written for the medium of electronic sounds and listened to what she came up with.

Similarly with Doctor Who the theme tune was well established. But there was always a request to 'tart it up' when new graphics were designed for the opening titles. Brian helped Delia with this a few times over the years, usually by adding swirls, whooshes and effects. But the essential musical parts remained.

Until someone suggested making a synthesiser version. Delia tried but the sounds on the Synthi 100, known as the Delaware, simply could not compete with the powerful effect of the original version made with real sounds and tape manipulation. I helped with mixing on this occasion and Brian lent his support as always. Delia did not want to submit this pale version to the producer Barry Letts but somehow it escaped and I believe it got used once on a foreign version of the show. Thankfully that was (almost) the end of the matter. It wasn't until nearly ten years later that Peter Howell made a new version of that iconic piece which to my mind is the best yet. It must have taken great courage to attempt this at all, bearing in mind the reluctance we all have to changing an old and familiar friend. To be fair to Delia the synthesisers available had advanced by leaps and bounds by this time but even so a great version, Bravo Peter!

Many years later the awful attempt by Delia with the VCS3 was somewhat mischievously released and I know Delia would have hated that. Everyone has incomplete tracks, demos and failed versions in the drawer and it is better that they stay there. I was not proud of the joint credit I was mistakenly awarded for that disaster.

While we are on the subject of disasters I was very lucky not to be asked to do a version of the great

'Journey of the Sorcerer' by the Eagles for the TV version of the Hitch Hikers Guide I don't know why they didn't want to use the original, maybe to do with obtaining rights. I was fortunately up to my neck in making the rest of the music and effects for the series at the time. They got Mike Oldfield to do a version and also Tim Souster. They ended up using the latter version. It is a terribly difficult track to cover, largely because of the very effective orchestral parts and I must say I prefer the original Eagles version because it is played straight rather than an attempt at comedy.

But returning to 1972 , the arrival of BBC2 and Local Radio meant that there were numerous requests for theme tunes. David Cain was locked into blockbuster radio programmes and John Baker had health problems. Desmond needed to find staff capable of doing this work. it must have been hard for Delia to have enthusiastic young people arriving just as she was going through a difficult phase and not at her most productive. Have you had the experience of opening a new piece of software only to find that using it seems like visiting an alien planet? The designers have joyfully put a brand new slant on something you were already familiar with. You are tempted to close it down and stick with the old version.

I imagine that this is how Delia felt in 1970, when a system she had helped to build suddenly looked like being drastically redesigned. All those tape recorders you see in the early Workshop films were mono. The hookups were relatively simple, but stereo seemed more complicated, although the record industry had been making stereo recordings for years. Synthesisers were poking their heads round the door, accompanied by young and enthusiastic new people. Delia was not naturally a management type, or she could have climbed the BBC ladder with ease. She was an artist and essentially a soloist. She needed a bit of technical help, but when 'set up' was free to roam in an electronic wonderland. In this new age the technology side of things looked as if it was in danger of taking over.

If she had been less vulnerable at that stage in her life, Delia would have coped and re-triumphed. But the combination of a chaotic personal life and change in the workplace was too much at the time. She was often said to have worked everything out before starting in the studio, but when I worked with her, Delia was great at busking it, experimenting and exploiting those 'happy accidents'. Adept at playing the machinery (if not hooking it up), and brilliant at moulding the sounds into something with extra magic. In jazz terms, it 'felt good'.

Her talent did not go unnoticed in the world of rock music. Ray Davies and Pink Floyd came to meet her and Paul Mcartney explored the possibility of using electronics for the recording of Yesterday. In the event he and George Martin used a string quartet for that but Sergeant Pepper was full of electronic sounds and I believe Delia's work may have inspired them to go in that direction. She was and is truly an inspiration, particularly to young women with dreams of making electronic music.

Brian Hodgson had a background in the theatre in the days of Rep. He came to the BBC as a studio manager and worked in radio drama until moving to the workshop. His contribution to Doctor Who is legendary, and he created some of the best known original sound effects in the world. The TARDIS is astill in use today. His work for drama is distinguished including 'The Machine Stops' directed by Philip Saville from the series Out Of The Unknown.

Brian left the workshop in 1973 to open his own studio with business partner John Lewis. Productions included 'The Legend of Hellhouse', John Schlesinger's section of 'Visions of Eight', the Munich Olympic Film and Derek Jarman's 'Tempest'.

Albums included 'Where are we Captain?', 'Zygoat' and 'New Atlantis' Ballet's were for Ballet Rambert, Royal Opera House, London Contemporary Dance Theatre and Peter Logan's Mechanical Ballet. When it was decided to create the new post of head of the workshop for Desmond, Brian returned as organiser and proceeded to revolutionise the facilities, eventually taking over running the workshop when Desmond retired. Events nobody could control led to the workshop closure in 1998. Brian's contribution to the success of the department over the years was enormous and his friendship and support to colleagues is hugely appreciated.

Malcolm Clarke joined the workshop staff a bit before me and I realise now that I never really got to know him. He and Dick Mills appeared to be great friends but now many years later talking to Dick I find that their friendship was more superficial than it had appeared. Malcolm was a visual artist, a trombone player and a highly practical individual. We were all at the stage of buying flats and houses in the early seventies and had to learn to do DIY for financial reasons. No matter how ambitious the project under consideration Malcolm would have already tackled it. Central heating, demolishing walls and putting in RSJs, you name it. I believe he even constructed a swimming pool later on and built a Bugatti car from spare parts.

He was the first at the workshop to do a Doctor Who music score, 'The Sea Devils', broadcast in 1972. and in the 80's he composed the music for five more Doctor Who series in the John Nathan-Turner era. His work on the radio version of Ray Bradbury's short story There Will Come Soft Rains received widespread acclaim. His approach was often experimental and always highly original, with many programmes for Radio 3. There were many producers who came back again and again to work with him.

Glynis Jones arrived in 1972, a trained musician with great sensitivity but at that time not very confident. She produced delicate textures often using tape techniques combined with the synthesiser available at the time. I remember that she was sometimes anxious about the process of making music to order, finding it difficult to relax and just allow it to happen. But she made some good things with a lasting quality such as Veils and Mirrors which appears on an album called The Radiophonic Workshop. In the end she decided that the workshop was not for her and left to do other things. I believe she arrived at the wrong time, when everything was changing but the direction wasn't clear. Five years earlier or later would have enabled her to develop her talents and shine.

Peter Howell came to the workshop in 1974 He had been a studio manager at BH and had previously had his own studio releasing albums of folk music with John Ferdinando which all these years later are highly sought after. For the next 23 years he not only composed memorable scores for 'The Body In Question', 'Doctor Who' and many more but also created programmes such as 'Inferno Revisited' for Radio 4, inspired by Dante's 'Inferno', as well as collaborating with Desmond Briscoe in his award winning productions. In 1980 he made a new version of the Doctor Who Theme which was highly successful and regarded by many as the best version so far. At the workshop Peter used synthesisers with enthusiasm but still experimented with tape techniques alongside the new technology. His work was and is meticulous. Desmond called him "the best pair of ears in the business". He stayed with the workshop until the end and is perhaps the longest serving composer of all of us. It was not my intention to cover the period after the workshop closed in this book but I should say that the band we formed to play at festivals over the last few years was based to a great extent on Peter's talent and showmanship and it is a joy to take part in that.

One day as I was walking out of the Langham opposite Broadcasting House I bumped into Roger Limb. I knew him from the Bush House days when he had joined us in our night time sessions with the band. He was by this time an announcer on BBC TV. I told him about the workshop and suggested he might be interested in it. He took up that idea and came on an attachment which eventually led to a very successful change of career. While at the workshop Roger was prolific. Many schools productions had his credit at the end for songs and incidental music. He scored eight series of music for Doctor Who and many other shows including The Box Of Delights. All this while playing jazz in his spare time. He is a great pianist and still gigging to this day. As if this wasn't enough he joined the BBC Club Gliding group and eventually became a gliding instructor. I mentioned earlier that the BBC club had sections for many pursuits which it was able to subsidise from the profits made by the bars which it ran. Almost all BBC buildings had a club bar nearby and unlike today drinking was an accepted feature of day to day programme making. The drinks were attractively below pub prices but even so profits were substantial and so expensive hobbies like sailing and flying became accessible to all and the club made Roger's gliding possible.

Desmond was delighted that Roger was happy to take a cut in salary to come to the workshop after being a TV announcer and used that fact in his negotiations to upgrade the pay of creative staff. Thanks Roger!

Elizabeth Parker came to the workshop in 1978 and was previously an SM at broadcasting house. When I was making the Music In Principle programmes she worked on one of the studio recordings. Later on she applied and after the usual attachments she got a permanent post at the workshop. She had taken a Masters in electronic music at the University of East Anglia and so was perhaps the first person actually qualified for the job! Hard working and focussed she was soon providing the special electronic effects for Blakes Seven and a Doctor Who story 'The Stones Of Blood'. But her musical talents soon came to the fore with the David Attenborough series 'Living Planet' followed by numerous radio and TV programmes over the next years including the Doctor Who adventure 'Timelash', Iris Murdock's 'The Bell and The Sea', Harold Pinter's 'Moonlight', 'King Lear', 'The Pallisers', Wordsworth's 'Prelude', and many more until she was the last composer to leave when the workshop was closed down in 1998.

I have only talked about the people who were at the workshop at the same time as I was, although of course there were many others earlier and later. I have tried to think of what we all had in common. Nearly all chosen by Desmond for a start. Fascinated by coaxing tunes out of temperamental machinery? Finding a bit of magic which communicates itself to a listener? That's it really, and when someone all these years later tells you they have been moved in some way by the music and sounds you have made, albeit just one component of a radio or TV production, there is no greater reward for your efforts.

Apart from the actual work of making shows there is a lot of effort behind the scenes. The BBC loves meetings and I have no problem with those with a specific purpose such as briefing for a show. I always hated routine meetings which were scheduled before an agenda had been set and went ahead even if there really wasn't anything to discuss. I tried to avoid these if possible because people still always managed to talk endlessly and achieve very little.

All of the studios in the workshop had an intercom connected to the office allowing the secretary or the organiser to listen in to the room and speak to the occupant. We always felt there was an element of Big Brother here because anyone in the office could listen in to private conversations.

One afternoon I was working on a new theme tune for the TV Schools programme Words And Pictures and had reached that exciting stage when the track felt good; all I wanted to do was to keep bashing it into shape. This stage is preceded by a series of dodgy ideas, self doubt, excuses, gratuitous diversions (my Mother was often surprised by a phone call during these moments), until the magic happens. Wild horses won't drag you away from this experience. I had the speakers up loud and my efforts at refining the tune to get it right contained all sorts of mistakes, unspeakable duff notes and general rubbish. All part of the 'creative process'.

I became aware of laughter in the background coming from the intercom. The rest of the staff were assembled in the office for that most sacred event the departmental mid monthly meeting. They had been listening to my activities before speaking to me to remind me that I was late. Embarrassing. I shouted "Sorry, deadline!" and carried on with the theme tune.

I suppose the BBC was no different from any other large organisation when it came to meetings. I remember going to my first 'planning meeting' at TV centre. The producer of the programme I was about to be involved in had nothing much to do at that moment so it seemed like a good idea to assemble everyone who would be working on the show to talk about it. I had thought it would be centred on the artistic side of things but quickly discovered that it was all about money and grabbing as much of the budget as possible for your particular department. Of course I didn't need to think about that because the workshop's costs were "under the line" and so I wasn't in competition with the others. One meeting I was unable to avoid was a 'Programme Review Board'. These were regular meetings chaired by the managing director of radio, at that time Aubrey Singer, with heads of departments. The object was to discuss the output of the networks, in this case over a bank holiday weekend, including specific programmes. Rockoco had cost a great deal of cash and was up for discussion, so as producer I was invited along. Quite a daunting experience to say the least. Heads of Radios One, Two, Three and various other departments were present. It seemed that the order of the day was to boast about your particular area and generally self aggrandise. When it came to my turn to discuss the programme I tried modesty, which of course didn't work. When Head of news Peter Woon was in the middle of talking up the contribution of his department and mentioning the news stories covered over the weekend, he was interrupted by Stephen Hearst, then head of Radio Three. "I'm interested that you use the word stories" he said with a mischievous glance. "I thought that the news was supposed to deal with facts!" Of course this meeting was just a grander version of the previously mentioned production meeting, essentially an opportunity to keep your end up and scrabble for a bigger share of resources.

Many years later after leaving the BBC I was invited to a meeting which was concerned with the right to use the name of the Radiophonic Workshop. The invitation described it as a "without prejudice Meeting" I was amused to find my cynical view was confirmed. Here was a meeting where it was actually decided in advance that nothing would be decided. The real truth is that when you are wrapped up with contributing to programmes, the organisation of the means to do it seems like a tedious detail. That's what the bureaucrats are for.

From the moment the workshop opened for business in 1958 there was an ongoing battle to get up to date equipment. I remember having a heated discussion with Desmond about tape machines. They had just spent a fortune on upgrading the reception area at the Maida Vale building which I thought should have been spent on the tools of the trade. Desmond said simply "It's not that kind of money".

Radio and Television were separate departments then with different systems of budgeting. Radio is obviously cheaper to make than TV, not requiring scenery, costumes, make-up, cameras, lighting, graphic design, location catering, etc. etc. In the early days budgets were divided into 'under the line' costs for BBC departments and staff and 'above the line' costs, money spent outside the BBC. Of course the 'under the line' part was benignly rationed to prevent producers hogging facilities.

So for instance the gramophone library was just there to be used as needed in productions. The same applied to the Workshop which led to a demand for music from departments which generally couldn't afford to hire freelance musicians, among them Schools, Further Education and Local Radio. It's hard to evaluate the merits of this state of affairs either way. Some say the market was distorted, others point to a huge amount of memorable material which would otherwise not have existed. A few years later the system was changed dramatically.

It is said that in 1986 a well known member of Margaret Thatcher's team 'received a mauling' during a current affairs interview at Lime Grove studios which led to a revenge campaign to shake up the BBC. And so the accountants moved in and things changed drastically over the next decade.

Long after I had left the BBC a huge re-structuring took place. Departments such as the workshop which had been 'under the line' now had to charge real money for their services, to be paid out of programme budgets. For a producer needing music the workshop was no longer a cheaper alternative. What is more, service departments including the the workshop would be charged for 'services' they used. So they got bills for accommodation, canteen facilities and even the reception desk at the entrance to the building. This resulted in their rates being less competitive than outside operators.. I was by that time outside the BBC and even though I paid rent and rates etc for my Hammersmith studio, I did not employ a commissionaire (why would I?) and my canteen was Marks & Spencers. To make matters worse the costs of setting up a recording studio had fallen dramatically. And so a whole generation of new composers materialised, capable of producing perfectly good material in their bedrooms for productions both inside and outside the BBC at knock down prices. At the time they were unkindly referred to as the 'Casio cowboys', so just as a few years before we had taken work away from freelance musicians, those at the Radiophonic Workshop suffered the same fate. They struggled on but in 1998, inevitably had to close down. Elizabeth Parker is said to have turned out the lights for the last time.

In our new incarnation touring as a 'band' we often talk about the fact that during our years at Maida Vale we weren't a band at all. We only met in the canteen or at the dreaded mid monthly meetings. The canteen was therapy for us with people of all ages discussing everything from car problems, (plenty in the 70s), to new babies, break ups, errant children, bereavement, last night's Morcombe and Wise, the latest scandal - almost everything except our music. When Karlheinz Stockhausen came to Maida Vale studios in the 60s Brian and Delia were agog to catch a glimpse of him. They hung around the staircase leading to studio one and were rewarded when the orchestra broke for lunch with the usual stampede for the canteen. The great man joined the queue and took a tray with everyone else. Straining to hear what he would order and thinking that it must at least be freshly prepared nectar they were disappointed to hear the words "savoury mince and mashed potatoes"

I have no idea what topics Karlheinz and his friends would have discussed over their savoury mince but on the radiophonic table DIY was a regular theme.

Most of us were plunged into home improvement projects for financial reasons, electrics, plumbing and kitchens with a bit of car maintenance for good measure. The canteen tables usually had a selection of pencil diagrams and sketches on the formica after lunch. Dave Young was always on hand to advise. A master of both theory and practice he once measured the pressure and head of water in my flat using a tyre pressure gauge and mental arithmetic.

On another occasion I brought in a dead TV set to see if it was worth fixing. Dave put it on a bench, took off the back and plugged it in to the mains. He then proceeded to touch various components with a finger to see if there was a voltage present. "No, no, AH! yes, no…"

A couple of minutes later he had found a resistor that had gone OC. (Don't ask), so grabbing a soldering iron he removed the offending component without switching off the set, found a replacement and soldered it in place with an impressive shower of sparks as the tv burst into life. Everyone met in the canteen except Desmond, I think he felt that as the boss he should maintain a certain distance. When Brian took on this role he was able to balance the managerial and social parts simultaneously. Different styles but whatever works is good.

I think I can say that I gave as much as could be expected of me in my work but I have to say that family came first. Holidays with the children were more important than taking on a plum job and in all honesty that means less than 100% devotion to work, which is not the case for many creative people. But this gentle brake can help prevent burn-out or going off the rails.

Deadlines were another important ingredient of sanity preservation. Broadcasting works on the clock and there was always a date beyond which it was impossible to go. That means that there is no room for the obsessive twiddling often found in creative activities.

Chapter 14: Moonlighting

When we joined the BBC we were told that we were not allowed to work for other organisations. However over the years this attitude relaxed a little and Desmond was sometimes asked to make effects for feature films. Brian and Delia provided music for modern Ballet and Theatre productions and John Baker also worked on film projects.

In fact the arrangement was formalised in a letter stating that it was allowed in spare time providing it didn't conflict with BBC work. I helped Delia and Brian with the sound for a couple of shows for the Greenwich Theatre, The Medea and Iris Murdoch's The Servants and the Snow. They launched themselves into the theatrical world with enthusiasm, a world Brian was already familiar with. They dressed appropriately for opening nights, Delia in flowing robes and Brian in a Black Jumpsuit, Pink shirt and 3 quarter length White Cardin Coat. While I trailed behind sartorially with the same sort of blue jeans I wear today. Their whole approach was glamorous, stylish and exciting. They were at the top of their game. My main memory is of the delicious whitebait served in the theatre restaurant.

Later I did two albums of music for EMI, recorded at Abbey Road studios These were with a co-writer Richard Belvue De Sylva, known as Sooty for reasons I never discovered. Every Wednesday evening we met to write material for these albums until the day arrived to record the real thing. Peter Mew was the engineer and I learnt loads from seeing him work. He combined solid technical know how with a talented artistic flair for balancing sound. He was also easy to get on with and had a sense of humour, much needed when working with us. There was a small canteen at the studio and when I selected a fish knife for my cod and chips I remarked that the BBC canteen did not have fish knives. No said Peter, you have THE fish knife. There is only one.

We recorded backing tracks, the parts for which I had prepared although my manuscripts were somewhat basic to say the least. No need to worry because Richard had hired amazing musicians to play. It was a mixture of pop standards and original material, the title of the first album was Supercharged. We spent a few evenings overdubbing the synthesiser parts using Arp equipment lent by that company free of charge. Our friend David Epps from BBC Further Education did arrangements for strings and brass which were added later.

I made a type of vocal gadget which produced a sort of Sparky's Magic Piano effect similar to the more modern Vocoders. A keyboard was fed into to a public address loudspeaker which instead of being connected to a horn was hooked up to a plastic tube, which reduced in size until the final diameter was about a quarter of an inch. This, somewhat unhygienically went in my mouth so that mouthed words came out with the sound of tunes played on the keyboard.

It must have sold one or two because they allowed us to make a second album a year or so later called Swag, with our own material and no cover versions. We had singers on this but otherwise it was similar to Supercharged, funky easy listening as befitted EMI's Middle Of The Road label. This time instead of using the home made gadget with the plastic tube we had the benefit of an EMI vocoder which made the vocal effect electronically. I even appeared on Blue Peter to demonstrate it which was fun if a bit nerve wracking.

I don't regret making the albums but I failed to raise my game for this wonderful opportunity, even though I took time off to fit it in. So much was going on at the time and I didn't see the wood for the trees.

Among other freelance work was making sound effects for a 1974 film called Count Downe, released as 'Son Of Dracula'. The movie was produced by Ringo Starr and featured Harry Neilson as Dracula. It was fun to get a glimpse of Rock and Roll during that production as was a session one evening at Air studios in Oxford street for a band called Medicine Head. I had met Tony Ashton at a session for The Sequence programme for Radio One. Once again a line up of wonderful musicians - and me. Tony was the producer. I played my Fender telecaster through a VCS3 synthesiser making sort of watery chords on a song called 'Rising Sun'. I think it got to number 11 in the charts. A bit later on in 1980 I did some work on a film called Dark Angel directed by Roger Christian which was the supporting film for the first release of 'The Empire Strikes Back'. The music was written by Trevor Jones who went on to a distinguished career as a movie composer.

Another bit of moonlighting was the mobile disco in the days before my time at the workshop. The band I mentioned earlier morphed into 'Gatecrasher" with drummer John and me. We built loudspeaker cabinets, amplifiers a twin turntable unit and lights. John favoured a robust construction approach which meant that the gear would not fit into a couple of cars. This led to the purchase of a Ford Transit van. Also we needed to rent a room in which to store the gear. We had cards printed and even a handout which proclaimed "…there is no time limit, we will play until the last guest leaves if you wish". How we regretted that. Last guests seem to have an enormous capacity for longevity.

One of the more rewarding gigs was at a centre for disabled children and young adults called Canada Villa. When we arrived our audience was waiting and eager to start. The love in the room was utterly touching with so many people in what most of us would consider to be desperate circumstances enjoying dancing in whatever way they could to the hits of 1969. There were quite a few parents present to help out and their devotion was obvious and moving. These children would not be flying the nest to go to Uni or wherever, there would be a lifelong commitment and a worry of what might happen at the end. But for a night everything was joy and the simple fun of dancing.

Chapter 15: Musicians

While at the workshop I often got musicians in to play alongside the electronics. The BBC symphony orchestra was based at Maida Vale and so it suited everyone very well. This required me to write out parts for them. Working with top musicians is daunting if you aren't classically trained. (Learn while you earn was my route). They don't suffer fools or pull any punches if something isn't right in the music. But I made several good friends including horn player Mick Baines, percussionists Terry Emery and Gary Kettel together with many others. I soon learned to double check everything before the session but even then there were always questions... But they were always generous and helpful in the end, not to mention the thrill of hearing a tune you have written played by wonderful musicians. I wasn't alone. Even very famous conductors and composers sometimes found themselves facing the merciless wit of the band. Leonard Bernstein visited Maida Vale to conduct the symphony orchestra on one occasion and arrived extremely late, while the entire orchestra sat around waiting in the studio. This is usually simply not done even by the most eminent conductors. He walked in with no apology and launched into instructions for which part he wanted to rehearse first. A voice from the back was heard to say "Car wouldn't start?" I am sure his scores were faultless and that the orchestra gave their all.

The profession can be cruel. A great trumpet player and a fine man John Wilbraham played for me a few times. He preferred to use a small piccolo trumpet most of the time and made a beautiful sound. His day job was with the BBC symphony orchestra and on a session with Piere Boulez conducting he had difficulty in getting an extremely quiet sound out of the instrument for a particular passage. After many attempts (in front of the entire orchestra), he was unable to achieve what was required by the Maestro. This had a lasting effect on him which was very damaging.

I have always loved the sound of the french horn. The Beatles song 'For No One' showed how a classical instrument can fit so well into a pop song. Alan Civil played on that and later on I was lucky enough to get him to play on some of my recordings. Another horn player Mick Baines was a great friend and also a 'fixer'. That is the person who assembles a band for a session. He played in the symphony orchestra as well as freelance film and pop sessions, so he knew everyone and they all loved him. Very sadly he died aged only forty.

While on the subject of great musicians, I was working in room ten one afternoon when a message came on the intercom "Would it be OK if Henry Mancini came in to see the Delaware?" He had just done an interview for Producer Bobby Jaye at the film unit down the corridor. He came in and was charming and unassuming. He didn't pretend to be up to date with electronics saying that his son took care of all that stuff. What struck me was that he was still interested in what other people were doing even after all his staggering achievements. What a privilege to meet him.

When we made that first album for EMI we had a budget for 'real' musicians. I wrote out the parts for the rhythm section, Alan Hawkshawe piano, Alan Parker guitar, Les Hurdle bass and Henry Spinetti drums. It was amazing to hear them play through my rather sketchy jottings and hear the powerful sound on the huge speakers in Abbey Road's famous studio two. We would later add my synthesiser parts. The last step was to add strings and brass. I got my friend David Epps to arrange and conduct those, way beyond my capabilities then. It was a real eye opener for me to fully appreciate just how good these musicians were. They could sight read anything and play it beautifully before going back to reading the newspaper, in between numbers. There were strict union rules about what could or couldn't be done at sessions which caused a great deal of angst at that time. It was easy to put a foot wrong and didn't exactly help the atmosphere. Fortunately things are much more relaxed and friendly now because the next generation have embraced the new technology and see it as a creative tool rather than a threat.

All of these experiences made me want to join the world outside the BBC and eventually I did just that. I had always wanted to start up my own studio. In fact, fifteen years earlier when frustrated by being stuck at

Bush House I had wandered round Soho and stupidly asked about jobs in a few sound facilities. I was told I was mad by the people there, many of whom would have given anything to get the stability of a job at the BBC. But fifteen years later during a restless phase in 1981 I decided to give it a go. If I hadn't got the green light from my wonderful wife Lynda it wouldn't have happened but she was always keen to be adventurous so the decision was made. We both knew that starting up on a shoestring would mean hours of hard work and that we would need to live closer to London. Up to then I had been commuting from Woking which consumed at least two and a half hours a day, an expensive waste of time. So in the space of about six months we had moved to south London and found a crumbling building available to rent in Hammersmith for the studio.

I handed in my notice to the BBC and was flattered that Auntie tried to persuade me to stay. But my mind was made up so that on the stroke of 12 o'clock on 31st December 1981 aged 34 I was no longer employed by the BBC.

As a child I had cuddled up next to the warm glow of our Bush radio set for Listen With Mother every afternoon at a quarter to two. A lovely lady called Daphne Oxenford read stories and transported her young listeners to the magical world of the imagination. I suppose my love for Auntie is as much wrapped up in that as later on working in the very studios where those programmes were made. Then the thrill of meeting the people who created early radio, such as Henry Hall one of the original band leaders who came in to do an interview. And later on producing a programme featuring the legendary guitarist Hank Marvin who influenced a generation of musicians.

When I recall the talented people I was lucky enough to be with I realise how much I learnt from them along the way. Thinking about this period of my life I wish that I had been able to appreciate it fully as it all happened. I suppose we can all say that because everything comes at once in your 20s and 30s. Marriage, children, houses, cars, work, holidays, all woven into the day to day routine.

I am so thankful for the opportunities I was given by that wonderful organisation and the friends I made there. The BBC is unique and during return visits after leaving I sense that much of what made it great still remains despite efforts by various politicians to break it up. The operational and production people I have met over the years still seem to have the same values as the ones in my day. Essentially a desire to work in an atmosphere focussed on doing the best possible job in the time available and not on competitive career building. But I suppose I would say that because I still have an emotional attachment and love for dear old Auntie. There seemed to be a common enthusiasm for broadcasting by everyone there. I suppose the thought of huge numbers of people listening to something you had contributed to is part of it. Fascination for the hardware, microphones, mixing desks and outside broadcast trucks is another. But I believe that because radio and TV have been such an intimate part of our home life practically from birth, we know what we are aiming at and that is what we have in common, ingrained from an early age.

As I write these words I am somehow transported back to those times so full of energy and fun with all the colourful characters springing back to life as if they had never left. When I have come to the end of a couple of hours of writing down these recollections and closed down my computer I find that for a short time my mind is actually back in those days when so much was happening but I was too busy at the time to appreciate how privileged I was.

I'm not much of a one for reunions but every now and again a group of elderly people gathers to stay the night in a hotel in the Worcestershire countryside. Gone are the cables mixing desks and tape recorders and there is no trace of the outside broadcasting point once hidden in the rose bushes. But the elegant facade of the building is unmistakably that of Wood Norton Hall. The conversation over dinner demonstrates how each of us have remembered a slightly different version of the time we spent there in 1966, but we all agree that the three month period was a major influence on our entire lives.

On January the first 1982 aged 34 and no longer a BBC employee I was off to begin a freelance career of my own and would not experience the agonies of the next few years which were lurking in the wings for those working for Auntie. My PK Studios adventure had begun. But that is another story...

Photo Credits

John Lightfoot:

Gogmagog + Merseybeat
PK + Synths
Festival Hal

Dick Mills:

Arp Odyssey
Suitcase Synthi
EMS VCS3

Creative Commons
(under CC by 2.0)

R/DV/RS:
Broadcasting House

Matt from London:
BBC Maida Vale
BBC Microphone

Special thanks to John Cavanah

THE BRITISH BROADCASTING CORPORATION

BROADCASTING HOUSE, LONDON, W.1

TELEGRAMS: BROADCASTS LONDON TELEX ★ CABLES: BROADCASTS LONDON-W1 ★ TELEX: 22182

TELEPHONE: LANGHAM 4468

Extension : 2675

Reference: 02/R/JMT   26th July, 1965.

P. Kingsland, Esq.,
Avon Cottage,
Ropley,
Nr. Alresford.

Dear Sir,

We have pleasure in offering you an appointment to the Unestablished Staff of the Engineering Division as a Technical Operator, subject to confirmation after your examination results are known.   Please inform us of your results as soon as they are known to you.

The appointment will be governed by the Staff Regulations, a copy of which is enclosed, and with reference to Clause 19 you are placed in the category of "Unrestricted" staff.   Changes in the Corporation's regulations affecting your terms and conditions of service may be promulgated by notices posted on notice boards on Corporation premises.   A formal Agreement for Service will be prepared for your signature after you have taken up this appointment, but a specimen copy of the Agreement is enclosed for your information and retention.

The first year of service will be probationary, and will commence with a residential training course at the Engineering Training Department. This course ends with a written examination and practical tests, success in both of which is essential if your services are to be retained.   Reports on work and conduct will be made each three months, and it is expected that these will give a postive indication of your suitability to have your appointment to the Unestablished Staff confirmed after one year.

The salary to be paid to you on taking up the appointment will be at the rate of £580 per annum, payable monthly in arrear by bank credit, and subject to satisfactory report will be increased:

to £705 p.a. on the first day of the month nearest your 19th birthday
to £830 p.a. on the first day of the month nearest your 20th birthday

thereafter annual increments will be in accordance with the general conditions of service for Grade D.   For the purpose of annual increments, if your birthday falls on a day between the 1st and the 15th inclusive then the increase will take effect from the 1st of that month.   If on the other hand your birthday is on the 16th of the month or later then the increase will take effect from the first of the following month.

On completion of two years service and reaching the age of 21 years you will become eligible for appointment to the Established Staff, subject to your work and conduct being to the full satisfaction of the Corporation, and to your health being considered satisfactory.   If you fail to reach the required standard you cannot expect to be retained in the service of the Corporation.   The Corporation has a contributory Pension Scheme, a brief summary of which is enclosed.   Until you become a member of the Corporation's Pension Scheme you will pay contributions to the State Graduated Pension Scheme.

An offer of employment

Gogmagog + Merseybeat

PK with favourite synths
Royal Festival Hall

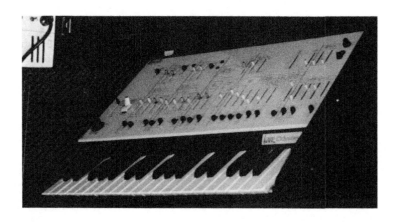

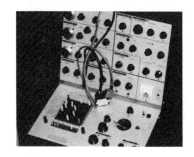

Arp Odyssey
Fender Telecaster
EMS VCS3.   Suitcase Synthi

Printed in Great Britain
by Amazon

30880616R00086